In 2000, Sandra Monger left her job as a registered nurse to follow her life-long passion for baking and cake decoration. She studied an array of sugarcraft courses under the tutelage of sugarcraft guru Stephen Benison, and in 2002 established her own business: Sandra Monger Exquisite Wedding and Occasion Cakes. Sandra became the City of Bath's leading wedding and celebration cake designer and the recommended supplier to some of the leading venues in the South West UK.

Sandra began teaching sugarcraft at Wiltshire College in 2007. She also designed and ran a range of popular sugarcraft and cake decoration courses at the City of Bath College as well as running her successful business. In 2012, Sandra was named Celebration Cake Maker of the Year at the British Baking Industry Awards.

Sandra's first book, 'Using Cutters on Cakes', was published by Search Press in 2014. Sandra lives in Bath, UK.

MODERN
GINGERBREAD

First published in 2020
Search Press Limited
Wellwood, North Farm Road,
Tunbridge Wells, Kent TN2 3DR

Suppliers
If you have difficulty in obtaining any of the materials and equipment mentioned in this book, then please visit the Search Press website for details of suppliers: www.searchpress.com

You are invited to visit the author's website:
www.sandramongercakes.co.uk

Publishers' note
All the step-by-step photographs in this book feature the author, Sandra Monger, demonstrating how to make and decorate gingerbread. No models have been used.

The projects in this book have been made using metric weights and volumes; the imperial weights and volumes provided on page 127 have been calculated following standard conversion practices. Where given, imperial conversions are often rounded to the nearest $\frac{1}{8}$in for ease of use; however, if you need more exact measurements, there are excellent converters online that you can use. Always use either metric or imperial measurements, not a combination of both.

Acknowledgements

I would like to thank the following people for their input and inspiration in this book: firstly, Robin Pakes, my husband, for his ideas and technical insight; my mum, Pauline, who inspired the *Picture Purr-fect* project; and Stephen Benison, who introduced me to gingerbread, for his help and support over the years.

MODERN GINGERBREAD

15 INSPIRING NEW IDEAS FOR BAKES AND CAKES

Sandra Monger

SEARCH PRESS

CONTENTS

Star and Bead Garland,
page 38

Wreath, page 58

Gift Boxes, page 82

Kransekake, page 86

Cookie Favours, page 42

Piped Snowflake Cookies, page 46

Bauble Cookies, page 50

Sharing Squares, page 54

Flower Planter, page 64

Christmas Tree, page 70

Gingerbread Street, page 74

Christmas Tree Cookie Cake, page 92

Wedding Cake, page 96

Picture Purr-fect, page 100

Gingerbread House, page 106

INTRODUCTION

Gingerbread is not just a warming winter treat; it can be enjoyed all year round! The gift ideas, delicious treats and charming and beautifully scented decorations in this book will brighten the home and bring joy to children and grown-ups alike. This is why I love working with gingerbread!

The fifteen step-by-step projects in this book show you how to bake, make, decorate and celebrate the heartwarming and creative wonder that is gingerbread. Think of this book as the beginning of your gingerbread journey. It will introduce and guide you through the tools, materials and techniques required for the projects, which you can then apply to your own creations. The book is also packed with recipes for gingerbread, delicious fillings, stunning edible adornments such as candied fruits and my favourite ginger cake.

We start by introducing the key skills such as cutting, piping and icing; these skills are developed through increasingly complex projects, all of which are designed to help you on your way to baking brilliance.

In this book I have attempted to use minimal specialist equipment; however, sometimes it is required. Much of this equipment can of course be used in other activities such as cake decorating and sugarcraft, but, wherever possible, alternative equipment in the form of everyday items is recommended.

So let's get baking, making, decorating and celebrating, and start your journey to gingerbread genius!

TOOLS AND MATERIALS

Before we start baking, making and decorating, let's have a look at some of the equipment, tools and materials we will be using. The projects in the book sometimes refer back to this section so it's worth familiarizing yourself with the equipment before you get started. This will make the projects easier and help you obtain the best results you can.

Making the dough

Baking gingerbread is at the heart of this book. To make a batch of gingerbread, you will need the following equipment and materials – these can be thought of as your 'basic toolkit', which can be applied to each of the projects in this book:

- **Kitchen scales, measuring spoons and jug** for weighing and measuring ingredients

- **Sieve** for sifting flour into a mixing bowl

- **Spatula** for stirring and mixing ingredients and removing mixtures from saucepans and bowls

- **Saucepan** for melting and combining ingredients

- **Tablespoon** for measuring, mixing and stirring

- **Mixing bowl** for mixing gingerbread ingredients

- **Ramekin** used to contain and mix small amounts of wet or dry ingredients before they are added to a mixture

- **Baking parchment or kitchen foil** for wrapping and storing raw gingerbread dough.

Rolling out gingerbread dough

To roll out your gingerbread dough, you will need:

- **Rolling pin**
- **Rolling spacers**
- **Baking parchment**
- **Silicone mat.**

These items also form part of your 'basic toolkit'.

ABOUT THE SPACERS

It is helpful to use a pair of spacers when rolling out gingerbread dough. These are used to achieve an even thickness and consistent bake on your gingerbread. Spacers can be made from everyday items such as a pair of wooden rulers or lengths of strip hardwood. I use lengths of strip hardwood that are approximately 3mm (⅛in) in depth. Most of the projects within this book require the gingerbread to be rolled to a thickness of 3mm (⅛in), although there are a few exceptions such as the *Picture Purr-fect* project on pages 100–105 and the appliqué projects such as the *Bauble Cookies* project on pages 50–53, where some of the dough is rolled out more thinly. This will be indicated in the individual projects.

ROLLING THE DOUGH

Gingerbread dough can be rolled out on baking parchment or a silicone mat before cutting. This makes it easier to transfer the unbaked pieces onto a metal baking sheet, helping to reduce any distortion of the cut-out shape. It is important to use a mat that is the same size as, or smaller than, your baking sheet.

Cutting gingerbread dough

Some projects in this book require readily available cutters. A set of **round and square metal cookie cutters** can be used along with a **sharp kitchen knife** to create a variety of shapes. **Shaped cookie cutters** such as Christmas baubles, snowflakes, lights, gingerbread people, animals and hearts are also useful.

A **scalloped edge frill cutter** is used for creating decorative edges.

Another useful tool is a **pizza wheel cutter**. The circular blade reduces drag on the dough, giving a cleaner cut that results in a smoother baked edge. A **sugarcraft wheel cutter** is useful for cutting out smaller details, particularly when using templates. A **parallel wheel cutter** is an adjustable wheel cutter with two blades, for cutting strips of dough, sugarpaste (fondant) and modelling paste.

A **paring knife** can be used for cutting and tidying fine details in dough. It is also useful for lifting and removing cut sections of rolled gingerbread.

Templates

Templates are a key feature of some of the projects in this book. A number of templates have been included in the back of the book (see pages 118–126); these can be photocopied or traced. Templates are best made from a heavy-grade paper or card. This makes them easy to cut, and they can be reused if they are handled carefully to reduce the risk of tearing.

Card can be bought from craft shops, although templates can also be made from the card used in food packaging, such as cereal boxes.

To make a template you will need:

- **Baking parchment** This can also be used as tracing paper.

- **Masking tape** to secure tracing paper or baking parchment.

- **Pair of scissors** If you are using paper or light card to make your templates, they can be cut out using regular scissors. You will get best results if the scissors are good quality, medium-sized and sharp.

- **Craft knife, metal ruler** and **cutting mat** These can be used to cut straight lines and are suited to cutting thicker cards. Care is needed as the knife is sharp and cutting curves requires practice as it is done freehand. A cutting mat will protect your work surface or table top.

- **HB pencil, soft pencil (B or 2B), ruler, pencil sharpener** and **eraser** These are essential if you are tracing the templates in this book or if you are drawing and making your own templates.

- **Pair of compasses** These are especially useful for creating the templates for the *Kransekake* project on pages 86–91.

- **Vegetable shortening (not shown)** This is applied to the underside of the template to prevent it from sticking to rolled-out gingerbread dough.

Baking gingerbread

To bake your gingerbread, you will need a flat **baking sheet**. If you have two of these sheets, it will help speed things up. A double-layer baking sheet is best as it is less likely to warp or buckle in the heat of the oven.

   You will also need:

- **Wire cooling racks** These are used for cooling baked gingerbread and for storing and transferring when a project is in progress.

- **Palette knife** This is useful for transferring baked gingerbread items onto cooling racks.

These items are also part of your 'basic toolkit'.

Decorating essentials

The decorating stage is when your gingerbread projects really come to life. While I have tried to keep specialist equipment to a minimum, some items are essential. The projects in this book use a range of readily available cutters.

- A **pizza wheel cutter, sugarcraft wheel cutter** and **parallel wheel cutter** can be used for cutting out shapes and strips of sugarpaste (fondant), modelling paste and thinly rolled gingerbread to be used as appliqué decoration. They prevent dragging so produce a cleaner-cut edge.

- **Piping nozzles** and **piping bag** (see instructions on page 17) These are essential tools when producing piped decorations.

- **Small acrylic rolling pin** and **non-stick rolling board** These are used for rolling out modelling and flower pastes and can be used in combination with a dusting bag (see instructions on page 17). The small rolling pin can also be used for lightly rolling over gingerbread in some of the baking techniques that will be demonstrated.

- **Flower cutters** for cutting decorative floral shapes.

- **Shape cutters** for cutting out whole shapes and parts of shapes.

- **Texturing tools** for embossing and creating details and patterns.

- **Scribing tool** for marking guidelines and points for piped decorations.

- **Edible felt tip pen** also used for marking guide lines and points for decorations.

- **Cocktail sticks (not shown)** for adding small amounts of paste colour to sugarpaste (fondant), modelling paste and royal icing.

- **Paper lollipop sticks** These will need to go in the oven when baking some of the projects in this book, so it is essential that paper lollipop sticks, not plastic ones, are used.

- **Airtight food storage bags (not shown)** prevent drying of stored gingerbread dough, sugarpaste (fondant) and modelling paste.

- **Artists' paintbrushes** can be used to apply small amounts of water to fix sugarpaste (fondant) and modelling paste, to neaten piped lines and dots and applying lustre and colours.

- **Masking tape** for fixing sheet materials and templates in place on your work surface.

- **Vegetable shortening** This can be applied to templates to prevent them sticking to gingerbread dough when cutting shapes. It is also useful to stop sugarpaste (fondant) and modelling paste from sticking to your hands, rolling boards and surfaces.

- **Cake boards** These are used for displaying your work.

- **Pencils, rulers, drawing compass, set square, scissors and heavy-weight paper** These are used for designing, drawing and cutting out templates.

- **Electric stand food mixer (not shown)** This can be used for a range of mixing purposes such as cake mixtures and fillings. It is particularly useful when making royal icing – use a K-beater with the mixer for mixing the royal icing (see page 25).

- **Dusting bag** used to create a light and even dusting on a rolling board or work surface to prevent sticking.

- **Non-toxic glue stick** for securing ribbon trims onto cakes and cake boards.

- **Food-grade cake dowels, cranked palette knife, icing sugar shaker, pastry brush, icing smoothers** and a **spirit level** for icing cakes.

- **Ribbons** and **decorative strings** Attach these around the edge of a cake board for an attractive finishing touch to your gingerbread houses or cakes.

Edible materials

- **Sugarpaste (fondant icing)** Sugarpaste (fondant) is used for decorating and covering gingerbread, cakes and boards. It can also be used for modelling if strengthened. It can be bought ready to roll, although this type of icing requires kneading; and comes in a wide range of colours. White sugarpaste (fondant) can be coloured with gels or paste food colourings to create specific tones and shades. It can also be textured and embellished to create decorative effects.

- **Modelling paste** Modelling paste is made by adding a strengthening agent to sugarpaste (fondant) so that it is pliable and elastic. It can be bought readymade or you can make your own (see page 25). It dries harder than sugarpaste (fondant) and is used where decorative items are required to hold their shape.

- **Strengthening agents** CMC powder (also known as tylose) and gum tragacanth powder are used to give decorative pastes pliability, stretch and strength, making them suitable for modelling. CMC powder is a synthetic cellulose gum while gum tragacanth powder is a natural substance derived from several species of shrub. Both powders take six to twelve hours to work when added to sugarpaste (fondant) so are best left to rest overnight once kneaded together. They will need to be stored in an airtight plastic bag to prevent them drying out.

- **Royal icing** Royal icing is used for piping decorative patterns and details and to fix decorative and structural items in position. It can also be diluted to create flood icing decorations (see page 35). Traditionally, royal icing included fresh egg whites as a binding and hardening agent, but I prefer to use Meri-white or pasteurized dried egg white as this is easier to measure, produces more consistent results and has a lower risk of contamination. Alternatively, egg-free royal icing can be made with aquafaba, the starchy water that is drained from canned unsalted chickpeas (see recipe on page 25).

- **Plain chocolate** Melted plain chocolate is used for gluing gingerbread together. It tastes great with gingerbread, which is a good enough reason to use it! It also sets more quickly than royal icing which is useful when making gingerbread structures, but can soften in warm temperatures, so after it has been used, the glued-together gingerbread parts should be kept cool.

- **Other edibles** Other edibles can be used for colouring, enhancing, patterning and embellishing. These include paste, gel and powder colours, natural flavourings, lustres and edible sprinkles, gems and silver balls or dragees. Clear spirits such as vodka can be mixed with lustre powders to form a suspension for painting onto the surface of gingerbread. The alcohol will evaporate. Alternatively, lustre powders can be mixed with a little water although it will take longer to dry and the finish may be less consistent. Candied orange slices, cinnamon sticks and star anise make lovely rustic fragrant decorations and embellishments.

Making a cornflour (corn starch) dusting bag

 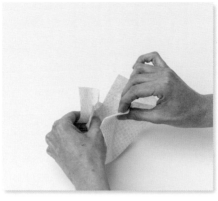 

1. Cut a 20cm (8in) square of clean lightweight kitchen cloth. Lay the cloth on a flat, clean surface and place a spoonful of cornflour (corn starch) in the middle of the square.

2. Gather up the corners of the square.

3. Secure with a length of string. Wrap the string twice around the bundle and tie it with a double knot.

Making a piping bag

Fabric piping bags can be bought readymade – some of these require a coupler to hold the nozzle in place. Readymade piping bags are useful if you will be using them a lot as they can be washed before reuse. However, if you prefer to make your own single-use piping bags, you can follow the instructions below.

1. Cut a right-angled triangle of baking parchment with the two shorter edges about 25cm (10in) in length and the longer edge about 30cm (12in) in length. Hold the triangle with the point facing down. Curl the top-right corner towards the point at the bottom and hold it in place.

2. Curl the top-left corner round to where the corner meets the base to form a cone.

3. Secure the cone by folding over the bottom point several times.

RECIPES

The following recipes make gingerbread that has a smooth, consistent surface and an even baked edge. The dough is easy to roll and can be coloured with paste food colours or made in a number of shades, substituting brown sugar for white to make a pale gingerbread or adding treacle or cocoa powder to produce darker shades.

Conversion tables for weights and volumes can be found on page 127.

Classic gingerbread

This classic all-purpose gingerbread recipe is ideal for cookies, treats and small structures. It produces an even baked surface and edge, can be re-rolled, refrigerated and frozen, although this recipe and the ones that follow are best used on the day they have been made.

Vegan gingerbread

Follow the classic gingerbread recipe and method but replace the same quantity of butter with dairy free vegan margarine and replace the egg with 1tsp of finely milled flax meal mixed with 25ml water. Allow the flax meal mixed with water to stand for 15 minutes before use – this allows the flax meal to swell in the water.

Ingredients

- 112g golden syrup
- 68g dark brown sugar
- 68g butter
- 300g plain flour
- 2tsp ground ginger
- ½tsp ground cinnamon
- 1 pinch of nutmeg
- 1 pinch of cloves
- ½tsp of bicarbonate of soda
- 3.75ml water
- Half a beaten egg – approximately 25g

Method

1. Weigh and measure the flour, bicarbonate of soda and spice. Mix together until the spice is evenly distributed, then sieve into a mixing bowl.

2. Beat the egg lightly.

3. Melt the golden syrup, dark brown sugar and butter together in a saucepan until all the sugar granules have dissolved. Do not allow to boil. Allow to cool a little.

4. Make a well in the middle of the flour and spice mix and pour in the melted syrup, dark brown sugar and butter. Add the egg and water.

5. Stir with a spatula to combine and knead to form a stiff dough.

6. Transfer the dough into an airtight plastic bag (or wrap in greaseproof paper) and allow to cool completely and rest at room temperature before use.

7. Preheat oven to 180°C / Fan 160°C / Gas mark 4.

8. Roll out and cut the gingerbread to the required shapes and thickness on baking parchment or a silicone mat using a cutter or template. Then gently slide onto a flat baking sheet covered with baking parchment. Bake for 8–15 minutes until evenly golden brown. (Note that baking times will depend on the size and thickness of the items you are baking.)

9. Once cooked, remove the baking sheets from the oven and allow to cool a little before transferring the items to a cooling rack with the help of a palette knife.

Tip

Use balls of unused gingerbread to weigh down the corners of the parchment if baking in a fan-assisted oven. This will help prevent the parchment from lifting which might distort the gingerbread as it is baking.

Pale gingerbread

This recipe makes a lighter gingerbread that uses white caster sugar. It can be used to provide variations in shade and is used when making coloured gingerbread. Like the previous recipe, it produces an even baked surface and edge, and can be re-rolled, stored and frozen.

Follow the classic gingerbread recipe and method (see opposite), but replace the same quantity of dark brown sugar with white caster sugar and omit the cloves and nutmeg.

Dark treacle gingerbread

Like the recipe for pale gingerbread, this darker gingerbread can be used to provide shade variation and has a deep and rich flavour.

Follow the classic gingerbread recipe and method but replace the same quantity of golden syrup with black treacle.

Rich chocolate gingerbread

Follow the classic gingerbread recipe and method but replace the same quantity of golden syrup with black treacle and replace 25g flour with 25g good quality cocoa powder.

Storing gingerbread and shortbread dough

The gingerbread doughs in this book can be stored in a refrigerator for three or four days if kept in an airtight food storage bag. They can also be frozen for several weeks if kept in an airtight bag. Shortbread dough can be stored for two days in the refrigerator.

Shortbread

Shortbread can be used to make light coloured inlays in gingerbread cookies. It also makes delicious cookies in its own right!

Ingredients

- 150g caster sugar
- 300g salted butter
- 400g plain flour
- 50g cornflour (corn starch)

Method

1. Preheat oven to 180°C / Fan 160°C / Gas mark 4.

2. Cream the sugar and butter together until it is light and fluffy.

3. Gently mix the cornflour (corn starch) into the flour until it is evenly distributed. Then sift into the creamed butter and sugar.

4. Mix to form a stiff dough, then sprinkle some flour onto a clean surface and knead the dough until it is smooth.

5. Roll out the dough and cut your desired shapes and place on a baking sheet covered with baking parchment.

6. Bake for around 12–15 minutes or until the edges are golden.

7. Remove from the oven and allow cooling a little before transferring to a wire cooling rack.

Coloured gingerbread

The beautiful golden colour of gingerbread is wonderful on its own; however, when it is used in combination with different coloured gingerbreads, you can create amazing effects. Certain colours perfectly complement the natural golden hues of gingerbread – red and yellow work particularly well, as do red and green.

Edible paste colours have been used to colour gingerbread in this book. These are the same pastes used in cake decoration and sugarcraft. The paste colours are added to the butter, caster sugar and golden syrup as they are being melted together. This disperses the colour well.

Add concentrated paste colour to one batch of pale gingerbread. I use the 'Sugarflair Extra' range as it produces vivid colours. However, I recommend that you do a little experimentation before you commit any colour to your gingerbread.

Colouring gingerbread

Method

1. Gather, weigh and measure your ingredients.

2. Mix together the flour, bicarbonate of soda and spice until the spice is evenly distributed, then sieve into a mixing bowl.

3. Melt the golden syrup, caster sugar, butter and ½tsp of your chosen food colouring together in a saucepan. Do not allow to boil.

4. Beat the egg lightly. Make a well in the middle of the flour and spice mix and pour in the egg and water.

5. Pour in the melted coloured syrup, caster sugar and butter mixture.

6. Stir with a spatula to combine.

7. Knead to form a stiff dough, then transfer the dough into an airtight food storage bag (or wrap in greaseproof paper) and allow to cool and rest at room temperature for 20–30 minutes before use.

Ginger cake

Although this is a book about gingerbread, I simply had to include a recipe for my favourite ginger cake, which is particularly delicious layered with caramel sauce (see opposite).

The recipe below is for the *Wedding Cake* on pages 96–99. You will need to bake three layers of cake for each of the three tiers.

Ingredients	13cm (5in) cake	18cm (7in) cake	23cm (9in) cake
Butter	120g	230g	380g
Light muscovado sugar	120g	230g	380g
Golden syrup	120g	230g	380g
Black treacle	120g	230g	80g
Self-raising flour	240g	460g	760g
Ground ginger	2tsp	4tsp	6tsp
Ground cinnamon	½tsp	1tsp	1½tsp
Chopped stem ginger	1tbsp	2tbsp	3tbsp
Eggs	1	2	4
Evaporated or whole milk	150ml	300ml	500ml
Approximate baking time	20–25 mins	25–30 mins	30–35 mins

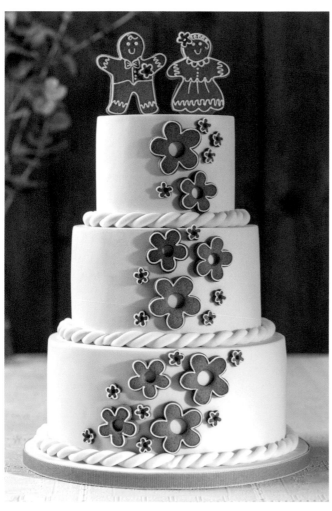

Method

1. Grease three round cake tins – 13cm (5in), 18cm (7in) and 23cm (9in). Line the bottom of each tin with a circle of baking parchment.

2. Preheat the oven to 180°C / Fan 160°C / Gas mark 4.

3. Gently melt the butter, sugar, golden syrup and treacle together in a saucepan. Do not allow to boil. Once melted allow to cool a little.

4. Mix the flour, ground ginger and cinnamon and sift into a mixing bowl.

5. Make a well in the flour and pour in the melted butter, sugar, golden syrup and treacle mixture. Add the stem ginger, beaten eggs and evaporated milk and combine thoroughly with a wooden spoon to form a uniform batter.

6. Divide the batter evenly into the three tins.

7. Place in the preheated oven and bake until the cakes have risen and are golden brown. A skewer inserted into the middle of the cake should come out clean.

8. Allow the cakes to cool in their tins on a cooling rack and cover with a clean tea towel to keep them moist. Allow to cool completely before removing from the tin and layering with caramel sauce.

CHRISTMAS TREE COOKIE CAKE

Use the ingredients table below to create the single-tier cake – remember that you will need to bake three layers of ginger cake to create a single tier.

Ingredients	15cm (6in) cake
Butter	210g
Light muscovado sugar	210g
Golden syrup	210g
Black treacle	210g
Self-raising flour	420g
Ground ginger	4tsp
Ground cinnamon	1tsp
Chopped stem ginger	2tbsp
Eggs	2
Evaporated or whole milk	280ml
Approximate baking time	25 mins

Sauces

Quite simply, these two sauces are a delight! Both caramel and chocolate make great dips for the *Sharing Squares* on pages 54–57.

CARAMEL SAUCE

Ingredients

- 2tbsp golden syrup
- 150g light brown sugar
- 30g butter
- 125ml double cream
- 2tsp vanilla extract
- Pinch of salt

Method

1. Melt the golden syrup, sugar and butter together in a saucepan and slowly bring to a rolling boil for one minute.

2. Turn off the heat and carefully add the double cream, making sure not to splash any of the mixture.

3. Turn the heat back on and gently bring to a rolling boil for one minute.

4. Remove from the heat and allow to cool thoroughly in a safe place where it cannot spill.

5. Once cool, add the vanilla extract and stir thoroughly. Finally, add a small pinch of salt to taste.

CHOCOLATE SAUCE (GANACHE)

Ingredients

- 100g good-quality milk or dark chocolate
- 100ml double cream

Method

1. Finely chop the chocolate and set aside.

2. Place the cream in a small saucepan and gently bring to the boil, stirring all the time.

3. As soon as the cream starts to boil, turn off the heat and add the chocolate. Stir until all of the chocolate has melted and combined to form a smooth glossy sauce.

4. Serve warm as a decadent dip for your gingerbread cookies.

Candied orange slices

Candied orange slices add jewels of colour and flavour to beautiful golden gingerbread. I have used them to decorate the gingerbread *kransekake* on pages 86–91. You can buy various candied fruits from confectioners, but you can easily make your own. Why not also try using sliced limes, lemon or tangerines for variety?

Ingredients

- Four small fresh oranges
- 900ml water
- 400g granulated white sugar

Method

1. Wash the oranges, then cut them into 3mm (⅛in) slices. Set aside.

2. Add 900ml water to a large saucepan and bring to a boil over a high heat. Add the orange slices. Boil gently for one minute. Carefully remove the orange slices and allow them to drain on a wire rack standing over a pan to catch the water.

3. Using a ladle, spoon out 500ml of the water used for boiling and discard the rest.

4. In a large pan, add the 500ml of reserved water and the sugar. Bring to a boil over a medium heat, stirring occasionally until the sugar has completely dissolved.

5. Turn the heat to medium-low and arrange the orange slices in a single layer if possible. Simmer for 45–60 minutes or until the rinds are slightly translucent. Swirl the slices in the pan every 15 minutes to make sure they are evenly coated with the sugar water and turn them over occasionally to check that they are not catching on the bottom of the pan. Check them regularly.

6. Transfer the slices to a cooling rack set over a large baking sheet. Let them sit for up to 24 hours or until dry.

7. If desired, dip the candied orange slices in granulated sugar. Use immediately or store them in an airtight container in the refrigerator for up to one month.

Melting chocolate

Break dark chocolate into small pieces and place in a glass mixing bowl. Place the bowl into a saucepan containing about 2.5cm (1in) of gently simmering water. Gently stir the chocolate until it has melted and there are no lumps, then turn off the heat. Put on oven gloves and remove the bowl so that the chocolate does not overheat.

If the chocolate sets, it can be re-melted. Make sure the saucepan does not boil dry, especially if you are re-melting the chocolate.

Carefully spoon some of the melted chocolate into a piping bag and snip the end to make a 2–3mm (¹⁄₁₆–⅛in) hole before applying. There is no need to use a piping nozzle. If the chocolate sets in the piping bag, it can be re-melted by placing in a microwave on the lowest setting for several seconds at a time, checking each time until the bag feels soft and the chocolate squeezes freely.

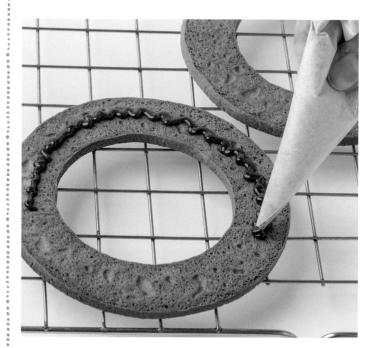

Royal icing

Royal icing can be used when piping decorations and for fixing pieces of gingerbread together. For vegan royal icing, the egg-white powder can be substituted for aquafaba, the starchy water in unsalted canned chickpeas.

Ingredients

- 454g icing sugar
- 70ml made-up pasteurized dried egg-white powder or aquafaba
- Two drops of lemon juice

Method

1. Mix dried egg-white powder with water according to the pack instructions and leave to stand for about half an hour before stirring. Strain to remove any lumps.

2. Sift the icing sugar into a clean and grease-free electric stand mixer bowl.

3. Pour in half the dried egg-white mixture or aquafaba and a couple of drops of lemon juice. Using a K beater, beat on the slowest speed until all the icing sugar is incorporated. Hold a tea towel tightly over the mixer and bowl when you first turn the mixer on, making sure it is free from any moving parts, to stop the icing sugar from exploding out of the bowl.

4. Slowly add the remaining egg-white mixture or aquafaba and continue mixing on a slow or medium setting until the icing forms stiff peaks and looks smooth and glossy. You may need to add a little more icing sugar or water to adjust the consistency.

5. Once the royal icing is mixed, transfer it into a clean bowl and cover immediately with a clean damp kitchen cloth. Keep the royal icing refrigerated when not in use and keep covered with a clean damp cloth at all times so that it does not skin over.

The consistency required will depend on your required use. Stiff-peak royal icing can be used for construction purposes and will dry more quickly. Softer-peak royal icing is better for piping decorations.

Royal icing can be kept covered and refrigerated for up to 48 hours.

Modelling paste

To make modelling paste, add one level teaspoon of CMC powder or gum tragacanth powder to 225g of sugarpaste (fondant) and knead well. Wrap in an airtight food storage bag and rest it overnight before use.

TECHNIQUES

Colouring sugarpaste (fondant) and modelling paste

Sugarpaste (fondant icing) and modelling paste can be coloured using edible paste colours.

1. Knead the sugarpaste (fondant) or modelling paste until it is warm and pliable. Then pick up a tiny amount of paste colour on a cocktail stick and transfer it to the sugarpaste (fondant) or modelling paste.

2. Knead the colour into the paste until you obtain an even colour.

Colouring royal icing

Royal icing can also be coloured using edible paste colour. Coloured royal icing is useful not only for decorative piping but also for matching the colour of gingerbread; using gingerbread-coloured icing to fix baked items together will make any joins less noticeable.

1. To colour royal icing, pick up a tiny amount of paste colour on a cocktail stick and transfer it to the icing.

2. Mix well with a palette knife or teaspoon.

Tip
Remember, you can always add colour but you can't take it away, so add it in small increments.

Coloured royal icing tends to be a little darker when it dries, so it is better to make it a little bit lighter than your desired shade.

Rolling gingerbread dough

To obtain an even, smoothly rolled sheet of gingerbread dough that is ready for cutting, you can roll the dough between two sheets of baking parchment, or between a silicone baking mat and a sheet of baking parchment.

Obtain an even thickness by using a pair of rolling spacers (see page 10) placed on either side of the dough. Let's roll with it!

Cut two sheets of baking parchment the same size or smaller than your baking sheet. If you are using a silicone mat cut just one sheet.

Lay a sheet of baking parchment or the silicone mat on a clean flat work surface and place the rolling spacers on it facing the direction you will be rolling. Leave sufficient space between the spacers for the gingerbread dough. Ensure that the ends of your rolling pin will easily reach over the spacers.

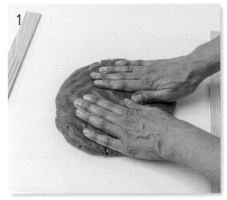
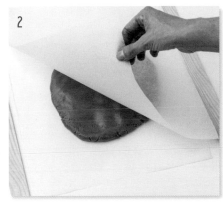
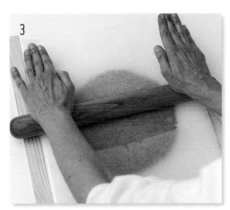

1. Place a piece of dough on the parchment or mat between the spacers and flatten it a little with your hand to make it easier to start rolling.

2. Place the remaining sheet of parchment over the dough.

3. Gently roll back and forth until the ends of the rolling pin come into contact with the spacers.

4. Continue rolling gently until the rolling pin rolls easily over the length of the spacers. Keep an eye on the baking parchment to make sure that it does not slip or crease.

5. Once the dough has been rolled to an even thickness, carefully peel off the top sheet of baking parchment to reveal a wonderfully smooth sheet of rolled gingerbread dough.

6. If the dough has rolled over the ends of the lower sheet of baking parchment or silicone mat onto the work surface, you can trim it off.

Cutting gingerbread dough

USING CUTTERS

Gingerbread can be cut with a variety of tools, depending on what shapes you require and what you are making. For defined shapes – such as squares, circles, stars, flowers and hearts as well as irregular shapes like animals or Christmas baubles, readymade cutters are a convenient and easily available means to obtain consistent results.

Select your cutters, ensuring they are clean and that any detailed sections are free of dried dough. Consider how many shapes you wish to cut out and how you might arrange the cuts on the rolled-out sheet of dough. Be careful not to cut the shapes too close together as the dough can spread when baking and the shapes can stick together. Conversely, do not cut too few as you could end up having to roll out and cut the dough again to obtain the desired number of shapes.

Cutting gingerbread dough

If you find that your shapes are too close together after you have removed the excess, simply slide the parchment sheet or mat with the cut shapes onto your baking sheet and place in the freezer for 20 minutes. After this you will be able to carefully reposition the shapes without them distorting.

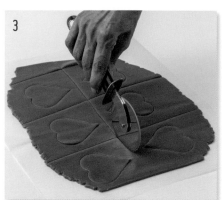

1. Hold your cutter above the rolled-out dough and press down evenly. To remove the cutter, lift gently and try not to wiggle it about as this could distort the shape.

2. Do not remove any dough from the sheet of parchment or mat at this time; simply continue to cut the next shapes, making sure they are evenly spaced and have room to spread as they bake.

3. Once all the shapes have been cut, slice the dough between the shapes into small sections with a pizza wheel cutter or paring knife. Take care not to cut into the shapes you will be baking.

4. Use the tip of the knife to lift out the sections until only the cut shapes remain.

5. Slide the sheet of baking parchment or silicone baking parchment onto a baking sheet ready for baking.

Templates

Where cutters are not available for a particular shape, you can use the templates provided at the back of this book. These have a wider creative scope and are essential for projects such as the gingerbread house (on pages 106–117), or where cutters of a desired size might not be readily available such as in the gingerbread *Kransekake* project on pages 86–91.

The templates included at the end of this book can be copied or traced onto paper, which can then be cut out and used as a template, or cut out, then drawn around on card to form a more robust template.

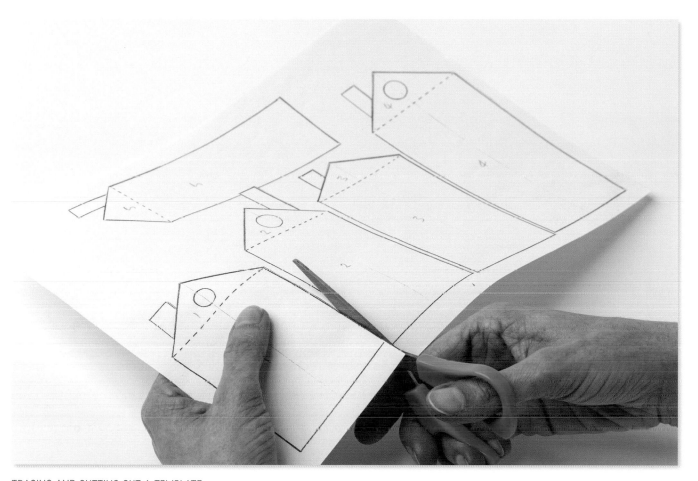

TRACING AND CUTTING OUT A TEMPLATE

1. Fix a sheet of tracing paper over the printed template with a few small pieces of masking tape and trace the shape using an HB pencil and ruler. Alternatively, you can photocopy the template directly from this book.

2. Remove the tracing paper and turn it over. Shade over the trace lines with a soft pencil.

3. Place the tracing paper shaded-side-down on your template card or paper and secure it with more masking tape.

4. Using a steady pressure, use an HB pencil to go over the lines you originally drew at step 1.

5. Remove the tracing paper to reveal a faint impression of the template. Carefully draw over the lines to make them clear. Label the drawn template with any information (such as 'top' or 'bottom') that is given on the template in the book before cutting out the template, to avoid any later confusion.

6. Cut out the template and store it flat, ready for use.

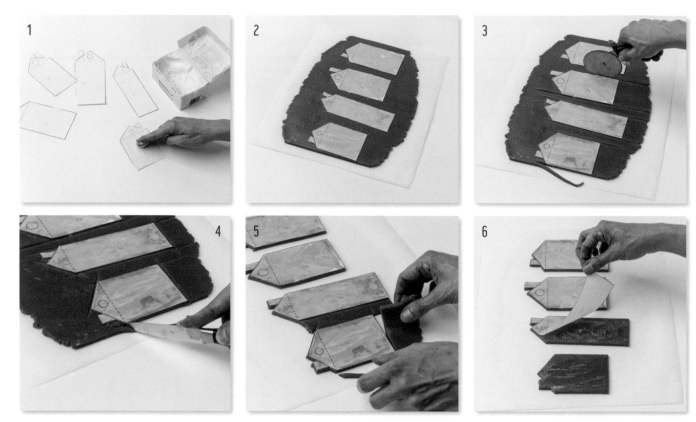

1. Roll out your gingerbread dough on a sheet of baking parchment or a silicone mat, as described on page 27. Evenly smear the underside of the template with vegetable shortening.

2. Place the template on the dough; make sure it is flat. Do not press it down as this could mark the dough and affect the quality of the baked surface.

3. Cut around the template with a pizza wheel cutter, taking care not to dislodge the template. Try to make the cut as smooth as possible using a single action.

4. Cut out any fine details with the tip of a paring knife.

5. Remove the excess dough.

6. Lift off the template, taking care not to mark the surface. If necessary, tidy any edges with the pizza wheel cutter or knife. Then slide the dough – on the sheet of baking parchment or silicone – onto a baking sheet, ready for baking.

Baking gingerbread

Baking is an essential process in making gingerbread. If you get the preparation, rolling and cutting right, the baking will be quite straightforward, with a bit of practice.

Baking times vary depending on the size and thickness of the gingerbread and the specifications of the oven you are using. The colour of the gingerbread as it is baking is the best guide to use; generally, when the edges have become a little darker than the centre, it is baked. Time-wise this can take 8–15 minutes at 180°C / Fan 160°C / Gas mark 4.

If you are baking a dark, coloured or chocolate gingerbread, it can be harder to tell when it is ready: it is best to familiarize yourself with how long the classic recipe printed on page 18 takes to bake in your own oven and use this as a guide.

Once your items are baked, allow them to cool a little on the baking sheet before transferring them with a palette knife onto a wire cooling rack to cool completely.

FUSE BAKING

Special effects can be obtained using a technique described as 'fuse baking'. Different coloured gingerbread doughs, or gingerbread and other doughs, such as shortbread, are cut, applied, arranged or inlaid together as a design or as parts of a pre-baked item. The doughs fuse together when they are baking to produce a single item.

Specific instructions for these techniques are provided in the relevant projects: *Cookie Favours*, pages 42–45, *Bauble Cookies*, pages 50–53, *Sharing Squares*, pages 54–57, *Flower Planter*, pages 64–69, the *Christmas Tree* parcel cake toppers on page 73, *Gift Boxes*, pages 82–85, *Picture Purr-fect* on pages 100–105 and the *Gingerbread House*, pages 106–117.

Covering a cake board with sugarpaste (fondant)

Covered cake boards are used to display some of the finished gingerbread projects in this book such as the gingerbread house on pages 106–117, the cakes on pages 92–99, and the Scandi *Flower Planter* project on pages 64–69. Covered boards give a neat, well-presented finish and provide a rigid base so that the items can be moved around easily without damage.

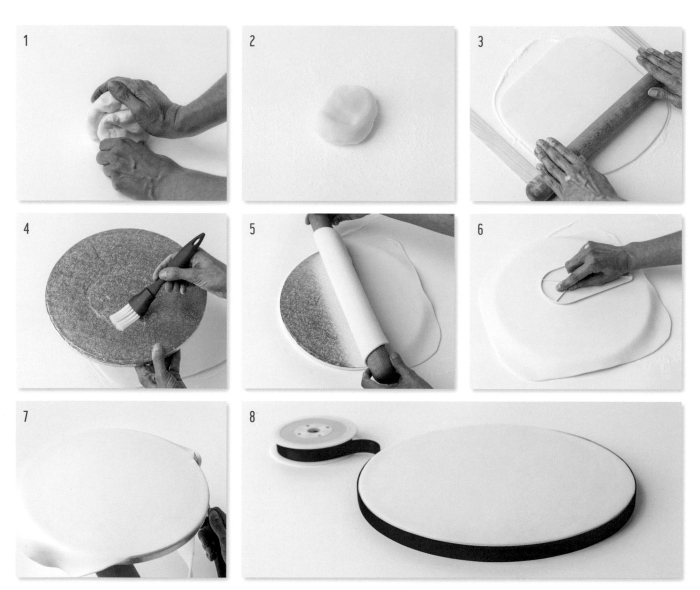

1. Knead the sugarpaste (fondant) on a clean work surface.

2. Dust your work surface with icing sugar, then place your kneaded sugarpaste (fondant) onto the dusted work surface, ready for rolling.

3. Roll out the sugarpaste (fondant) to the required size using the spacers to give an even thickness.

4. Lightly brush your cake board with cooled boiled water.

5. Pick up the sugarpaste (fondant) over the rolling pin and lay it evenly over the cake board.

6. Smooth the top of the sugarpaste (fondant) with a smoother and brush off any excess icing sugar.

7. Pick up the board from underneath and rest it on one hand. Slice off the excess sugarpaste (fondant) from the sides of the board using a knife. Allow the sugarpaste (fondant) to firm up for a couple of days before using it to display your finished gingerbread project.

8. Trim the board edge with your chosen ribbon: fix it in place with non-toxic glue.

Piping

Piping is an essential decorative and constructional technique for many of the projects in this book. It is used to apply royal icing to fix together baked items, and to add colour and detail to your gingerbread – bringing it to life.

Start by making some piping bags, using the instructions on page 17, then fill them with royal icing.

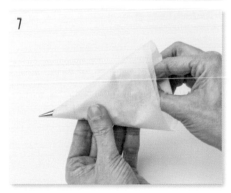
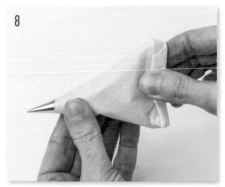
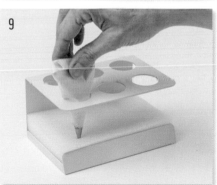

1. Spoon in a small amount of royal icing of the desired consistency so that the bag is no more than half full.

2. Fold over the corners of the open end of the bag,

3. Fold over several times until the icing has been squeezed into the pointed end of the bag.

4. At this point the piping bag can be used as it is if you are using it to fix items together. Simply snip off the pointed end to leave a 2mm (⅟₁₆in) hole.

5. For decorative piping, a piping nozzle is required. Take a second piping bag and cut off the pointed end to about a third of the length of your desired piping nozzle.

6. Fix your nozzle onto the end of the filled piping bag.

7. Place the filled bag into the second, ensuring that the pointed end is cut and firmly positioned inside the piping nozzle.

8. Fold down the open end of the outer bag as before, then gently squeeze it so that the icing comes out of the tip of the piping nozzle.

9. While the bag is not in use, stand it in a piping bag stand or a glass with a damp cloth or sponge in the bottom to prevent the icing in the tip of the nozzle from drying out and blocking the nozzle.

PIPING DESIGNS

Individual projects in this book will demonstrate a range of different piping techniques. Most of the piped decorations will include line, dot, dash, bead and snail's trail bead piping techniques.

All of the piped patterns shown below have been created with a number 1.5 piping nozzle and varying amounts of squeeze pressure. I hold a piping bag between my thumb and fingertips and sometimes use my other hand as a steadying support as seen on page 61. Piping requires practice and experimentation, so practice on a piece of scrap gingerbread to perfect your technique, concentrating on piping consistently sized elements and spacing.

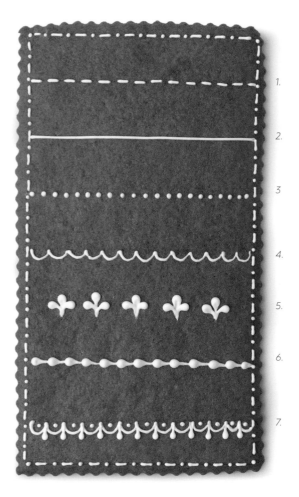

1. A line of dashes To form a dash, touch the piping nozzle tip to the gingerbread, squeeze gently to apply a small amount of pressure while drawing the nozzle a little way along. Then stop squeezing and drag the nozzle in the same direction for 1–2mm (1/16in) to break the icing string before lifting the nozzle away.

2. A straight piped line To form a piped line, touch the piping nozzle tip to the gingerbread and apply steady and even pressure. Lift the nozzle away gently so that a string of icing is suspended between the gingerbread and the nozzle. Once this has reached the desired length, cease pressure and gently lower the nozzle to touch the gingerbread and lay the piped line on the surface.

3. A series of tiny dots Touch the nozzle to the gingerbread, apply a little pressure and lift immediately upwards. Repeat to form a line of dots. The piped dots will have peaks which can be carefully flattened with a small, damp artists' paintbrush to make them neater.

4. A scalloped line Touch the nozzle to the gingerbread, apply steady and even pressure while drawing the nozzle along as if writing a continuous line of letter 'U's, forming a series of joined curves and peaks.

5. Fleur-de-lys Touch the nozzle to the gingerbread and apply pressure to form a small bead of icing. Release the pressure and drag the nozzle towards you to form a tail. Repeat this on either side, angling the tails towards the centre to form a fleur-de-lys pattern.

6. Bead piping (snail's trail) Touch the nozzle to the gingerbread. Apply pressure to form a small bead of icing, release the pressure and drag the tail along. At the end of the tail, apply pressure to form another bead and drag another tail. Repeat this technique to form a piped beaded line.

7. Drop and dot scalloped line This combines a scalloped line, dots and beads. Start by piping a scalloped line, then adding the dots. Complete the pattern by piping beads under the points of the scalloped line and dragging their tales to the points.

Flood icing

Flood icing is a decorative technique where the space inside a piped outline of royal icing is 'flooded' with diluted royal icing to produce a smooth, firm covering. Always use freshly made royal icing to achieve the best results and finish.

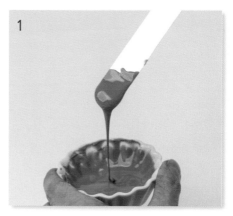

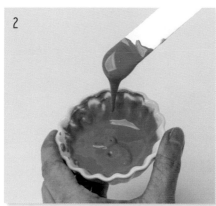

PREPARING YOUR ICING

Fill a piping bag with a number 1.5 piping nozzle in place with freshly made normal piping consistency royal icing of the required colour and place in a piping bag stand.

1. Make your flood icing by place the required amount of freshly made royal icing in your chosen colour in a small bowl. Thin it with a small amount of water or egg-white solution; add the liquid a drop at a time, gently stirring to incorporate.

2. While adding the liquid, keep checking the consistency. To do this, pour a thin line of royal icing with your spoon back into the bowl in which you have mixed the icing, and slowly count to ten. When the line takes ten seconds to settle and disappear, leaving a smooth, flat surface, the flood icing is the correct consistency.

3. Pour the flood icing into an unsnipped piping bag, taking care not to overfill it, then ensure that you fold over the wide end securely.

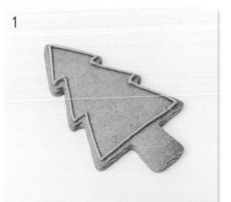

PIPING AN OUTLINE AND FLOODING

1. Pipe your chosen outline, using the piping bag with the number 1.5 nozzle.

2. Take the piping bag containing the flood icing and hold it with the pointed end facing upwards and snip a 1–2mm (1⁄16in) hole across the point. Flood inside the outline, using a gentle pressure. Once you have flooded along the outline, flood inwards in a spiral formation.

3. Once you have reached the centre, place the bag in the holder and use a scribing tool or cocktail stick to pop any air bubbles and gently work the flood icing into any unfilled gaps or corners.

4. Allow to dry on a flat surface. This can take several hours – I advise that you leave the icing to dry overnight.

The trees on top of the Christmas Tree Cookie Cake (see pages 92–95) have been decorated using the flood icing method.

THE PROJECTS

STAR AND BEAD GARLAND

This project uses cutters and coloured gingerbreads along with ribbon and rustic jute string. The gingerbread decorations and beads are threaded together to make a wonderful fragrant hanging decoration.

❋❈❈❈❋

You will need:

- Your 'basic toolkit' (see pages 8, 10 and 13)
- 1 batch of classic gingerbread dough (see page 18)
- ½ batch each of red, green and yellow coloured gingerbread dough (see pages 20–21)
- Royal icing
- 4½m (15ft) rustic jute string
- 1½m (5ft) of 7mm- (¼in-) wide rustic ribbon
- 60mm star cutter
- 25mm star cutter
- 30mm, 20mm, 10mm circle cutters
- Piping bag
- Number 2 piping nozzle

> ## Tip
> This garland can be made longer or shorter as required; you will need extra string and ribbon to lengthen the garland.

1. Cut out and bake six whole star shapes and six star shapes with a smaller star removed from the centre.

2. Cut out and bake forty-nine, assorted colour 30mm circles with 10mm holes cut out of the centres; and eighteen assorted-colour 20mm circles with 10mm holes cut out of the centres.

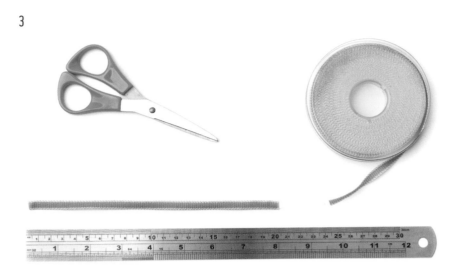

3. Cut six 20cm (8in) lengths of rustic ribbon.

4. Fold each length of ribbon in half and iron it flat.

5. Fill a piping bag with white royal icing and attach the number 2 piping nozzle. Pipe a little dot of royal icing on the topmost point of each solid star and fix a ribbon loop in place.

6. Pipe dots of royal icing on all of the points of the solid star and on top of the ribbon. Fix the star with the cut-out centre on top. Allow the icing to dry hard. Make sure you don't add too much icing as it will show in the centre hole.

7. Once the star and ribbon loop are firmly attached and the icing has dried, thread three of the small bead circles onto the loop. Repeat this for all of the stars.

8

9

10

11

8. Take the full length of rustic jute string and tie a large knot 25cm (10in) from the end, by tying several smaller knots in the same place. The large knot needs to be big enough so that the gingerbread beads cannot pass over it.

9. Thread seven of the large gingerbread beads in assorted colours onto the long length of the string and tie another large knot to hold them in place.

10. Make two smaller knots about 1cm (⅜in) apart, 5cm (2in) on from the last large knot, then thread on one of the stars.

11. Make another large knot 5cm (2in) on from the star and repeat steps 8, 9 and 10 until all of the beads and stars are threaded.

Tip

The garland can be hung and displayed but avoid allowing the gingerbread to touch wall coverings or furnishings as the butter and colour within the gingerbread may stain the surfaces.

COOKIE FAVOURS

These pretty cookies use cutters of assorted shapes and sizes to create fuse-baked inlays and lacy patterns that are combined with a fine piped white outline to add a delicate edge. These cookies make lovely favours for weddings, parties or as gifts. Alternatively, you can add name tags to your cookies to make wonderful place settings for your Christmas table.

You will need:

- Your 'basic toolkit' (see pages 8, 10 and 13)
- 1 batch of classic gingerbread dough (see page 18)
- Half a batch of shortbread dough (see page 19)
- 65mm round fluted cookie cutter
- 20mm petal cutter
- 20mm five-petal flower cutter
- 20mm heart cutter
- 7mm heart plunger cutter
- 15mm and 5mm circle cutters
- Piping bags
- Numbers 3 and 1.5 piping nozzles
- White royal icing, piping consistency
- Cookie bags and decorative ribbon

1. Roll out a sheet of classic gingerbread dough using 3mm-deep spacers to give an even thickness on baking parchment or a silicone mat. Repeat to make a smaller sheet of shortbread dough. Gather the tools and cutters ready for use.

2. Using the round fluted cookie cutter, cut several cookie shapes, leaving at least 2–3cm (¾–1¼in) space between each shape. Use your choice of smaller cutters to remove sections of dough from each gingerbread cookie, which can be inlaid with shortbread or left empty to form various patterns.

3. To inlay some of the sections, use the appropriate cutter to cut the matching shape in shortbread dough.

4. Carefully position the matching shortbread shape into the space.

5. To build the pattern further, remove a shape from the shortbread dough.

6. Fill this space with a matching shape in gingerbread dough.

7. Finally, dot in small circles around the outside of the cookie using a number 3 piping nozzle to give a lacy effect.

8. Repeat this process using your choice of cutters to give different patterns. Bake the cookies for 8–12 minutes until lightly golden brown on the edges.

9. Once the cookies have cooled completely, pipe a scalloped line (see page 34) to follow the outline of the cookies, using a number 1.5 piping nozzle.

10. Once all of the cookies have been outlined and the royal icing has dried hard, place each cookie into a cookie bag and tie with a pretty ribbon of your choice.

PIPED SNOWFLAKE COOKIES

These pretty snowflake cookies feature pastel-coloured royal icing,
piped lines and assorted-sized dots to help you develop your piping
skills. Why not create your own patterns and use different colours using
the simple method shown in this project?

❦

You will need:

- Your 'basic toolkit' (see pages 8, 10 and 13)
- 1 batch of classic gingerbread dough (see page 18)
- 75mm snowflake cookie cutter (or use the templates on pages 118–119)
- Pencil
- Scribing tool
- Edible felt-tip pen
- Piping bags
- Five number 1 piping nozzles
- Pastel pink, peach, green, blue and yellow piping consistency royal icing
- Artists' paintbrush
- Templates (see pages 118–119)

1. Cut out and bake a number of gingerbread snowflake-shaped cookies. Use a pencil to trace the snowflake patterns at the back of the book (see pages 118–119) onto squares of baking parchment.

2. Place the traced pattern over the cookie and using a scribing tool prick a series of faint dots to mark out the pattern (a). Alternatively, use an edible felt-tip pen to mark out your chosen pattern, drawing directly onto your gingerbread (b).

3. Fill five piping bags with each of the different colours of royal icing and fit each bag with a number 1 piping nozzle. Set aside in a piping bag stand, as shown on page 33.

4. Depending on your chosen pattern, select your choice of coloured royal icing and outline the cookie using the faint pricked markings as a guide.

5. Pipe straight lines, each in a different colour, to form the star in the centre of the cookie.

6. Pipe three contrasting coloured dots at the end of each line, one large and two small. The size of dot can be controlled by applying more or less pressure when piping. Use a damp artists' paintbrush to flatten and smooth any peaks on the dots.

7. Pipe a dot in the centre.

8. Pipe small and large dots in various contrasting colours to radiate out from the centre following the pricked out markings, to build up the pattern.

9. Continue piping dots until the pattern is complete. Allow the icing to dry hard.

10. Repeat the same process for the other snowflake patterns, using your choice of colours.

10

BAUBLE COOKIES

These double-sided hanging bauble cookies make lovely, fragrant tree decorations. In this project, thinly rolled gingerbread in different shades is used as appliqué, which fuses with the cookies as they bake to create textured decorations.

You will need:

- Your 'basic toolkit' (see pages 8, 10 and 13)
- 1 batch of classic gingerbread dough (see page 18)
- Half a batch of dark treacle gingerbread dough (see page 19)
- Half a batch of pale gingerbread dough (see page 19)
- Bauble cookie cutters, assorted shapes and sizes
- 50mm and 20mm star cutters
- 25mm and 7mm heart cutters
- 5mm circle cutter
- Parallel wheel cutter with wavy and straight cutting wheels
- Paring knife
- Stitch wheel embosser
- Numbers 1 and 3 piping nozzles
- White royal icing, piping consistency
- Piping bag
- Assorted narrow-width ribbons

1. Roll out a sheet of classic and treacle gingerbread dough on baking parchment or a silicone mat using the 3mm spacers. Cut out your bauble shapes. As the cookies are double-sided, you will need two of the same shape for each bauble to sandwich together.

2. On a separate sheet of baking parchment or a silicone mat, roll out small amounts of classic, treacle or pale gingerbread dough to a thickness of 1mm (1⁄16in). This will be used to cut out assorted shapes to apply as appliqué.

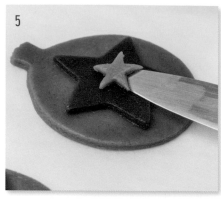

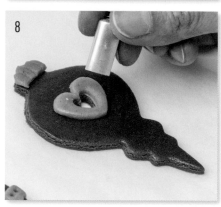

3. Cut out your choice of stars, hearts and wavy edged ribbons from gingerbread dough.

4. Cut a straight edge along one of the sides of the thinly rolled gingerbread dough. Using just the top part of a bauble cutter, cut out several bauble tops. You will need these shapes in both colours.

5. Build up the appliqué by layering opposing-coloured gingerbread dough shapes onto the bauble shapes and positioning an opposing-coloured bauble top in place.

6. Texture the bauble tops with a paring knife to mark a series of embossed lines.

7. Decorate some of the baubles with ribbons of opposing coloured gingerbread dough cut with a parallel wheel cutter using a straight and wavy cutter set 5mm (³⁄₁₆in) apart. Further decoration can be added by cutting out tiny holes along the ribbon with a number 1 piping nozzle.

8. Cut-out heart shapes can be added, and the centre of the bauble cut out with a small heart cutter.

Tip

As the appliqué gingerbread dough is rolled very thin, it can be placed into the refrigerator for 15–20 minutes to firm up before use. This will make it easier to handle.

Why not add a little bow for variation?

9. Emboss a stitch pattern onto some of the ribbons for extra texture using the stitch wheel embosser.

10. Once all the baubles are decorated, bake and allow to cool ready for assembly.

11. Finally, cut 20cm (8in) lengths of your chosen ribbon and sandwich two identical bauble cookies together using royal icing and the number 3 piping nozzle, following the instructions on page 40 (*Star and Bead Garland*).

SHARING SQUARES

These gingerbread tiles, or sharing squares, are inspired by the beautiful Portuguese tiles known as *azulejos*. They are inlaid with shortbread, red and treacle gingerbread, and can be cut and baked individually or together in a large square to make a wonderful centrepiece that can be shared with friends. The tiles are especially good freshly baked and dipped into caramel or chocolate sauce (see page 23 for the recipes).

You will need:

- Your 'basic toolkit' (see pages 8, 10 and 13)
- 1 batch of classic gingerbread dough (see page 18)
- Quarter batch of red coloured gingerbread (see pages 20–21)
- Half a batch of treacle gingerbread dough (see page 19)
- Quarter batch of shortbread dough (see page 19)
- Ruler
- Long bladed knife
- Paring knife
- 40mm four-petal flower cutter
- 35mm circle cutter
- 10mm circle cutter
- Caramel or chocolate sauce (ganache) for dipping (see page 23)

Tip

Plan ahead! These sharing squares can be rolled out ready for baking the day before they are needed and stored flat in the refrigerator, then baked ready for serving when your friends arrive.

1. Roll out a large sheet of classic gingerbread dough on baking parchment or a silicone mat using the 3mm spacers. Mark out a 23cm (9in) square using a ruler. Do not remove the excess.

2. Use the ruler to measure and mark nine 7.6cm (3in) squares.

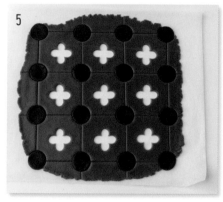

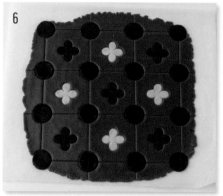

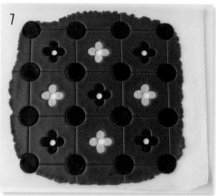

3. Next, remove circles of gingerbread dough at all the corners of all the squares with the 35mm circle cutter.

4. Roll out small amounts of treacle and red gingerbread dough as well as a small amount of shortbread dough on separate pieces of baking parchment or a silicone mat. Use spacers to ensure they are all the same thickness. Next, use the 35mm circle cutter to cut out circles of treacle gingerbread dough and inlay these circles into the spaces already cut.

5. Use the 40mm four-petal flower cutter to lift out flower shapes from the centre of each square.

6. Cut the same sized flower shapes from red gingerbread dough and shortbread dough and inlay these shapes in alternate spaces.

7. Using the 10mm circle cutter, lift out a small circle of dough from the centre of each flower.

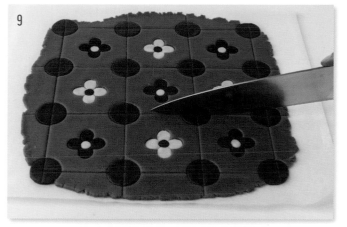

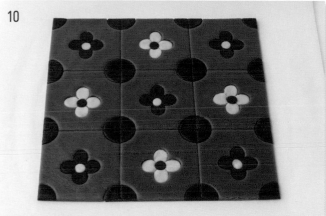

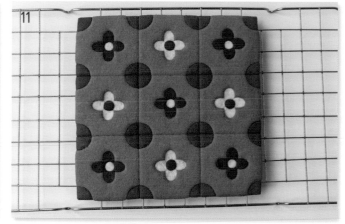

8. Cut the same sized circles in alternating colours and inlay them into the spaces.

9. Cut the outline and squares again to cut the treacle circles.

10. Remove the excess gingerbread dough from the sides. Slide the baking parchment with the sharing square onto a baking sheet and bake until lightly golden brown for around 12 minutes.

11. Once baked, allow the square to cool a little on the baking sheet, then carefully remove from the baking paper or silicone mat and cool completely on a wire rack.

Tip

If you wish to bake separate tiles, refrigerate the finished square for 15–20 minutes to firm up the dough, making it easier to handle without distorting the shapes; then cut and separate each square before baking. Ensure that there is sufficient space between each tile to allow for any spread when baking.

WREATH

This stylish and modern gingerbread wreath can be used as a beautifully scented eye-catching decoration, or as a striking and delicious cake topper or table centrepiece.

You will need:

- Your 'basic toolkit' (see pages 8, 10 and 13)
- 2 batches of classic gingerbread dough (see page 18)
- Half a batch of red gingerbread dough (see pages 20–21)
- Small amount of white modelling paste
- White royal icing
- Gingerbread-coloured royal icing (see below)
- 50mm, 35mm, 25mm, 20mm, 10mm circle cutters
- 100mm round cookie cutter
- Pizza wheel cutter
- Parallel wheel cutter with wavy edge wheels
- Stitch wheel embosser
- Artists' paintbrush
- Paring knife
- Number 1.5 piping nozzle
- Piping bag
- Length of wide ribbon or hessian at least 48cm (19in) long
- Stiff double-walled corrugated card
- Rose gold lustre powder
- Clear food-grade spirit (such as vodka) for mixing lustre powder (optional)

> ## Tip
> Gingerbread-coloured royal icing can be made by mixing tiny amounts of brown, yellow and orange paste food colouring to white royal icing.

1. Roll out a large sheet of classic gingerbread dough on baking parchment or a silicone mat using spacers. Cut a 23cm (9in) circle either by making a template or by cutting around a 23cm (9in) cake tin or plate using a pizza wheel cutter. Then cut out and remove a 100mm (4in) circle of gingerbread dough from the centre using a cookie cutter. Next, cut about eight 50mm (2in) circles, thirteen 35mm (1⅜in) circles, ten 25mm (1in) circles, eighteen 20mm (1³⁄₁₆in) circles and ten 10mm (⅜in) circles in roughly even quantities from red and classic gingerbread dough (cut out a few extra of each for luck!). Then cut a 20mm (1³⁄₁₆in) circle out of five of the 50mm (2in) circles to form offset rings. Bake all the shapes and allow to cool.

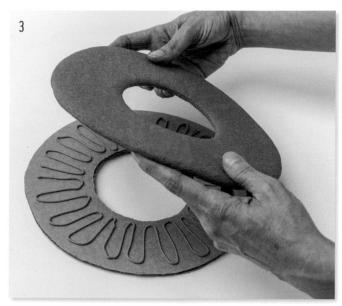

2. Draw around the baked 23cm (9in) circle of gingerbread and the 10cm (4in) circle hole on stiff corrugated card.

3. Fix the gingerbread to the card with gingerbread-coloured royal icing.

4. If you intend to hang the wreath, pass the hessian ribbon through the hole until both ends are of equal length and fix in place with royal icing. Stitch the ends together.

5. Decorate a number of the red gingerbread circles with a series of offset lines using white royal icing and a number 1.5 piping nozzle.

6. Pipe a number of classic gingerbread circles with a broken line outline using the same piping nozzle.

7. Roll out some white modelling paste to a thickness of 1mm (¹⁄₁₆in) on a surface lightly dusted with cornflour (corn starch). Cut some wavy ribbons using the parallel wheel cutter, with the wavy wheels set 5mm (³⁄₁₆in) apart.

8. Emboss the ribbons with a stitch wheel cutter.

9. Decorate a number of the larger and smaller circles of classic gingerbread with the wavy ribbons, fixing them in place with a little water applied with a clean artists' paintbrush.

10. Trim the ends of the ribbons with a paring knife.

11. Mix some rose gold lustre powder with some clear food-grade spirit or water if preferred and paint the upper surfaces of the remaining circles.

12. To complete, assemble the wreath by fixing and layering the decorated circles in a random fashion with gingerbread-coloured royal icing.

FLOWER PLANTER

This fun Scandi-style flower planter uses a number of techniques including appliqué, piping, baking and construction.

You will need:

- Your 'basic toolkit' (see pages 8, 10 and 13)
- 3 batches of classic gingerbread dough (see page 18)
- Half a batch of red gingerbread dough (see pages 20–21)
- Quarter batch of green gingerbread dough
- Half a batch of chocolate gingerbread dough (see page 19)
- 70mm, 30mm, 20mm, 15mm circle cutters
- 70mm, 65mm, 35mm, 30mm five-petal flower cutters
- 20mm petal cutter
- 10mm heart cutter
- 150mm- (6in-) long white paper lollipop sticks
- Paring knife
- Pizza wheel cutter
- Piping bags
- Numbers 1.5 and 3 piping nozzles
- White royal icing, piping consistency
- White royal icing, flood consistency
- Pliers
- Metal skewer
- 30cm (12in) round white iced cake board for display (see page 32)
- Decorative ribbon
- Food processor (optional) or rolling pin and food storage bag

1. Roll out a sheet of classic gingerbread dough on baking parchment or a silicone mat using the 3mm spacers. Cut out the backs of the flowers using either 70mm round cutters or 70mm five-petal flower shape cutters. Position a lollipop stick centrally onto the shape and press it lightly into the dough.

2. Roll out another sheet of classic gingerbread dough as before and cut out the leaf shapes freehand using a pizza wheel cutter. These leaves are about 4 × 5.5cm (1⁹⁄₁₆ × 2³⁄₁₆in). Press a lollipop stick lightly into the leaf shape as before. Cut smaller, thinly rolled green gingerbread leaf shapes – 3 × 4.5cm (1³⁄₁₆ × 1¾in) – and place on top of the leaf and lollipop stick. You will need six leaves in total.

3. Roll out a further sheet of classic gingerbread dough and cut out the fronts of the flowers. Each flower is made up of two identical shaped cookies so cut the same shape and number of cookies to match the backs. Next, roll out a small amount of red gingerbread dough to a thickness of 1mm (¹⁄₁₆in) on a separate sheet of baking parchment or a silicone mat. Cut out five 20mm petal shapes to apply as appliqué to the flower fronts.

Tip

As the appliqué gingerbread dough is rolled very thin, it can be placed into the refrigerator for 15–20 minutes to firm up before use. This makes it easier to handle.

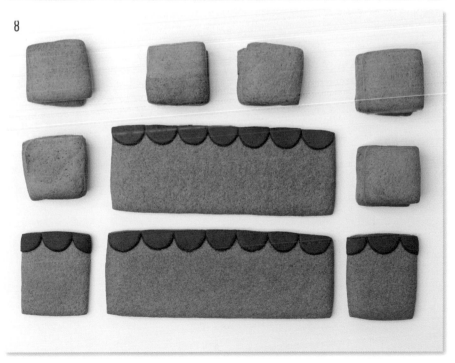

4. Position the red petal shapes centrally onto each petal of the larger flower shape.

5. Remove a 30mm circle out of the centre of the shape.

6. Remove small circles from each of the red petals using a number 3 piping nozzle.

7. Alternative flower designs can be made by using the same technique with the other cutters shown and described in the tool list above.

8. Next roll out and cut the planter panels: cut two rectangles of classic gingerbread dough 200 × 80mm (8 × 3⅛in) in size and two smaller rectangles 70 × 80mm (2¾ × 3⅛in) in size. Cut out ten 30mm circles of red gingerbread dough. Cut each circle in half and position along the top edges of the rectangles. You will also need eighteen 50mm- (2in-) square gingerbread cookies to place inside the planter once assembled, and a 200mm- (8in-) square sheet of baked chocolate gingerbread, which will be used to crush up for the crumb soil. Bake all of these items for 12–15 minutes and allow to cool completely.

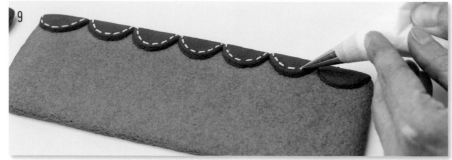 

9. Decorate the planter panels by outlining the red scallops with a broken white piped line using a number 1.5 piping nozzle.

10. Decorate the flower fronts by outlining the red flower with a broken line and piping a fleur-de-lys (see page 34) inside each petal. Other piped decorations can be created with different patterns.

11. Decorate the leaves by piping straight lines to form veins onto the inner green section.

12. Once the decorative icing has dried, assemble the flowers. Pipe royal icing on the back of each flower front and around the central hole to form a barrier when the flood icing is added to the central hole.

13. Sandwich the front and back of each flower together.

14. Flood the flower centre with white flood icing and allow to dry. Repeat this process and decorate the other flowers in your choice of style.

15. Next, assemble the planter on the white iced 30cm (12in) round cake drum. You may need to trim the base and side edges of the planter panels with a serrated knife if they are not straight. Pipe a generous line of gingerbread-coloured royal icing onto the bottom panels to fix them to the drum and side joints of the panels to fix them together. Once fixed, allow the joints to set.

16. Layer the square gingerbread cookies inside the planter and fix them in place with royal icing.

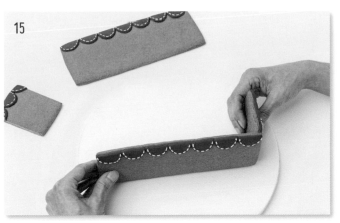

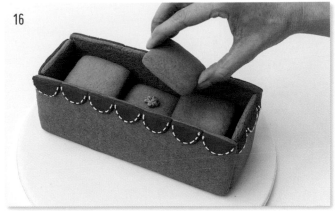

17. Break up the chocolate gingerbread and either place in a food processor and pulse until you have fine crumbs or place the gingerbread in a bag and beat it with a rolling pin to form crumbs. Then spoon the crumbs onto the top of the cookies inside the planter.

18. Make holes in the crumb soil and the cookies below for the lollipop stick flower stems to sink into, using a skewer, then position the stems.

19. Trim some of the excess length from the leaf stems with pliers and repeat step 18 for the leaves. Finally, trim the base board edge with a ribbon of your choice.

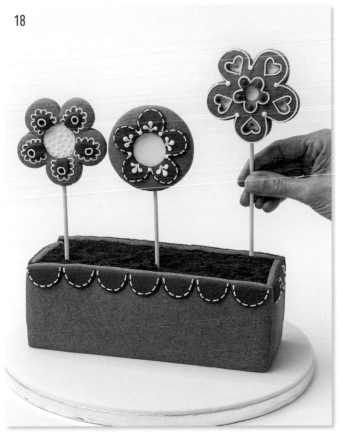

CHRISTMAS TREE

This charming gingerbread Christmas tree makes a lovely table centrepiece, mantel decoration or topper for your Christmas cake. For extra Yuletide cheer why not make accompanying gingerbread parcel cupcakes to stand around the tree.

✳✿✿✿✿✳

You will need:

- Your 'basic toolkit' (see pages 8, 10 and 13)
- 1 batch of green gingerbread dough (see pages 20–21)
- Half a batch of classic gingerbread dough (see page 18)
- Quarter batch of red gingerbread dough (see pages 20–21)
- Sugarcraft wheel cutter
- Paring knife
- Long serrated knife
- Scribing tool
- 30mm star cutter
- 10mm circle cutter
- 35mm square cutter
- Green and gingerbread-coloured royal icing
- Silver sugar balls (dragees)
- Piping bags
- Number 2 piping nozzle
- 180mm (7in) round white iced cake board
- 15mm- (⁹⁄₁₆in-) wide ribbon to trim the display board
- Templates (see pages 119) – you will also need a template for the base, formed of a 15cm- (6in-) diameter circle with three equal, intersecting lines across (see page 73, step 7)

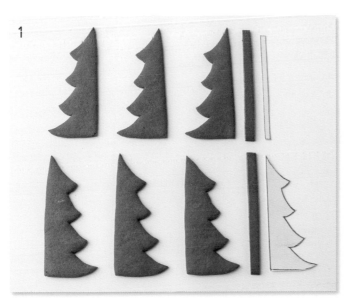

1. Copy or trace the branch and tree trunk templates supplied on page 119 and cut them out. Roll out the green gingerbread dough on baking parchment or a silicone mat using 3mm spacers. Cover both sides of the template for the tree branches and one side of those for the tree trunks with vegetable shortening. Next, use a wheel cutter and the tree branch template to cut three left tree branch panels, then turn the template over and cut three right panels. Finally, use the tree trunk template to cut the two tree centre strips.

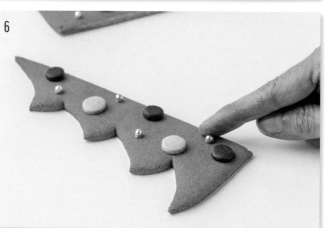

2. Roll out a sheet of classic gingerbread dough and a smaller sheet of red gingerbread dough. Next, cut a 15cm- (6in-) diameter circle from the classic gingerbread dough using a paper template. Cut out two 30mm star shapes and about forty 10mm circles. Then cut about forty 10mm red circles. Bake all the sections, the base and the decorations and allow to cool. You will also need 55 to 60 edible silver balls (dragees).

3. Pipe a wavy line of green royal icing onto one of the tree trunk strips and sandwich or fix both strips together. Allow to dry hard. You may need to trim the strips with a serrated knife first to ensure the sides are straight.

4. Fix the two star shapes together with a small amount of white royal icing.

5. Carefully trim the bottom and inside edges of the tree branch panels so they are straight and at right angles.

6. Decorate both sides of each tree panel with the small gingerbread circles and silver balls, fixing them in place with green royal icing, allow them to dry. Ensure that you set aside one or two classic gingerbread circles for fixing the star in the final stages.

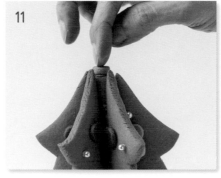

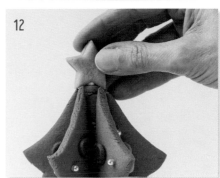

7. Lay the base template over the gingerbread base. With a scribing tool, lightly prick out six dots, one on each line 40mm (1⁹⁄₁₆in) out from the centre of the circle. Mark the centre point as well.

8. Lightly scribe lines between the dots to use as a guide when positioning the panels.

9. Assemble the tree by first fixing the tree trunk to the circular base with green royal icing. Ask someone to hold it in place for you.

10. Next, using the scribe lines as a guide, fix the green tree panels to the trunk and the base with green royal icing.

11. Fix one of the set-aside 10mm circles to the top of the tree with green royal icing. Add an additional circle if the trunk isn't quite long enough.

12. Fix the star in place with gingerbread-coloured royal icing.

13. To make gingerbread parcels to decorate cupcakes, cut a 35mm (1³⁄₈in) square and a 30mm (1¼in) star of classic gingerbread dough for each cupcake. Cut off two of the points from a cut-out star shape and position on top of a square. These will fuse while baking. Bake and allow to cool. Pipe lines and bows onto each parcel in your choice of colours. Fix the parcels on top of cupcakes to complete the project.

GINGERBREAD STREET

GINGERBREAD STREET

Not just the best address in town but also a colourful and charming decoration that will brighten any shelf or mantelpiece.

This fun project uses templates and a range of decorative techniques to bring the gingerbread to life.

You will need:

- Your 'basic toolkit' (see pages 8, 10 and 13)
- 3½ batches of classic gingerbread dough (see page 18)
- White royal icing
- Pink, lilac, blue, pale turquoise, peach, red, green and white modelling paste
- Silver sugar balls (dragees)
- Paring knife
- Long bladed knife
- Serrated knife
- 25 × 15mm rectangle cutter
- 10mm and 5mm circle cutters
- 45mm carnation cutter
- 5mm five-petal flower plunger cutter
- Pizza wheel cutter
- Pencil and ruler
- Set square
- Rolling pin
- Non-stick rolling board
- Cornflour (corn starch) dusting bag
- Vegetable shortening
- Sheet of heavy paper or light card
- Scissors
- Piping bags
- Number 1.5 piping nozzle
- Artists' paintbrush
- Rigid display board of your choice (for example, a rectangular wooden chopping board)
- Small jars or bottles (to support the gingerbread)
- Templates (see pages 120–121)

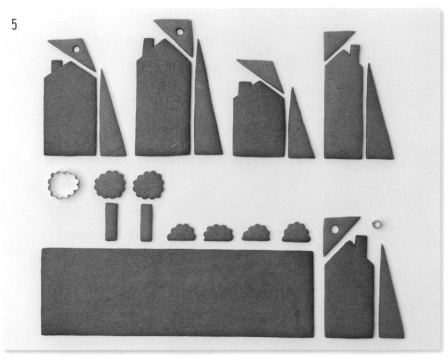

1. Trace or copy the templates at the back of the book (see pages 120–121). Make sure that you also trace the dotted cut lines that separate the roof from the walls and chimney.

2. Cut out the outline of the templates but do not cut along the dotted cut lines.

3. Roll out a sheet of gingerbread dough on baking parchment or a silicone mat using the 3mm spacers. Cover the underside of all the templates with vegetable shortening and arrange on top of the gingerbread. Cut around the house front and back support templates using a long bladed knife or pizza wheel cutter. You may need to re-roll and cut several times to complete all of the pieces.

4. Cut along the dotted cut lines on the templates to remove the chimneys and separate the triangular roofs from the walls.

5. Re-roll the gingerbread as before. Apply a little more vegetable shortening to the templates. Arrange on the gingerbread dough and cut out the triangular shapes with a long bladed knife or pizza wheel cutter. Remove the excess dough and remove 10mm holes from three of the triangles. Cut out four 45mm carnation shapes, cutting two equally in half, and two small 50 × 15mm (2 × ⁹⁄₁₆in) rectangles. Finally, roll out and cut a 370 × 115mm (14⁹⁄₁₆ × 4½in) rectangle of gingerbread dough for the base. Bake all the gingerbread pieces and allow to cool.

6. Pipe the outline of the chimneys and the triangular roof sections in your own design, using a number 1.5 piping nozzle and white royal icing.

7. Fix the triangular roof sections to the houses with royal icing. Allow to dry.

8. Lightly dust a clean work surface with cornflour (corn starch) and roll your choice of coloured modelling paste to a thickness of 2mm (¹⁄₁₆in). Use the appropriate-sized template to cut out a rectangle of paste to cover the front of the house.

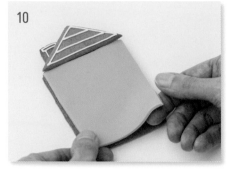

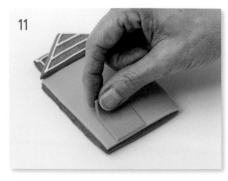

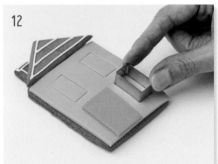

Tip

Some of the doors may need to be a little bigger or smaller depending on the size of the house.

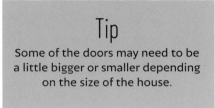

9. Brush a little water onto the surface of the house.

10. Fix the modelling paste in position.

11. Roll out a small amount of contrasting-coloured modelling paste. Cut out a 35 × 25mm (1⅜ × 1in) rectangle for the door; fix it in place with a little water.

12. Emboss rectangular window shapes using a 25 × 15mm rectangle cutter.

13. Pipe the windows and glazing bars using the embossed markings as a guide.

14. Pipe an outline around the door with white royal icing and fix a silver sugar ball (dragee) for the door knob with royal icing.

15. Fix the gingerbread carnation shapes onto the 50 × 15mm (2 × ³⁄₈in) rectangular tree trunks with gingerbread-coloured royal icing. Roll a small amount of green, white and red modelling paste as before and cut out a number of shapes using the carnation cutter from the green paste, then cut two of these shapes in half for the shrubs. Cut out a number of red 5mm (³⁄₁₆in) circles from the red paste and a number of 5mm (³⁄₁₆in) flowers using the flower plunger cutter.

Fix the green carnation shapes onto the trees and shrubs with a little water and decorate the trees with the red circles and the shrubs with white flowers, fixing them in place with a little water.

16. The flowers can be cupped by pressing down on the plunger when the flowers are ejected from the cutter directly onto the shrub.

17. Repeat the same process for all of the houses using different-coloured modelling pastes and different piped patterns.

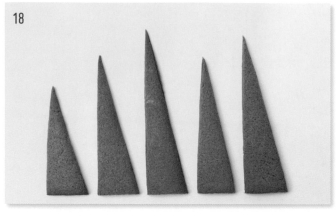

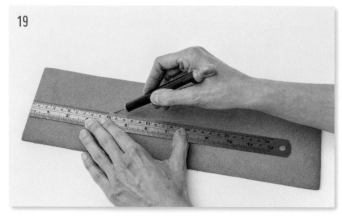

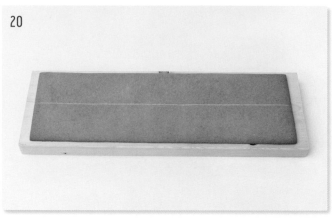

18. Trim the bottom and sides of each of the back supports and the bottom of each house with a serrated knife and ensure they are all straight.

19. Scribe a straight line with a ruler in the middle of the gingerbread base to give you a guide as to where the houses will be positioned.

20. Fix the gingerbread base to a suitable rigid display board with royal icing and allow to dry.

21. Fix the appropriate-sized back supports onto each house with gingerbread-coloured royal icing.

22. Fix each house to the base along the scribed line with gingerbread-coloured royal icing and support until dry with a small jar or bottle.

23. Fix the trees and shrubs in place with gingerbread-coloured royal icing. Allow to dry before moving the finished street.

GIFT BOXES

These eye-catching gingerbread jars and boxes are a great way to present a gift, whether it's cookies, sweets or something very special.

These projects use cutters to form the sides of the boxes and pots and combination baking to create the decorative lids.

The technique used in this project can be easily adapted to create a wide variety of shaped boxes and jars while the fuse baking techniques used in earlier projects can be adapted to make different lid styles and designs

You will need:

- Your 'basic toolkit' (see pages 8, 10 and 13)
- 1 batch of classic gingerbread dough (see page 18)
- 1 batch of red gingerbread dough (see pages 20–21)
- 5mm, 25mm, 50mm, 65mm, 85mm circle cutters
- 5mm, 40mm, 60mm and 75mm heart cutters (optional)
- Gingerbread-coloured royal icing

1. To make the lid, first roll out a rectangle of classic gingerbread dough approximately 170 × 130mm (6¾ × 5⅛in) and the same-size rectangle of red gingerbread dough on baking parchment or a silicone mat using the spacers.

2. Lay and align the classic gingerbread dough on top of the red gingerbread dough.

83

3. Gently roll up the rectangles of dough to show a spiral pattern at each, ensuring there are no gaps. Then place the roll into the refrigerator for an hour until very firm.

4. Neaten the roll by cutting off the end, then cut six 3mm- (⅛in-) thick discs from the roll using a sharp smooth bladed knife.

5. Cut a 50mm circle of classic gingerbread dough and position the discs around it.

6. Gently press the shapes together so that there are no gaps.

7. Place a piece of baking parchment over the top of the shape and roll very lightly with a rolling pin to give it an even thickness without distorting or enlarging it.

8. Roll out a sheet of classic dough and a sheet of red gingerbread dough on baking parchment or a silicone mat using spacers. Cut out five 85mm (3⅜in) circles of classic gingerbread dough, then remove a 65mm (2½in) circle from the middle of four of the shapes. Repeat this process with the red gingerbread dough but remove 65mm (2½in) circles from all five of the shapes. Cut a 5mm (³⁄₁₆in) and a 50mm (2in) circle of classic gingerbread dough and a 25mm (1in) circle of red gingerbread dough. Bake all of the pieces and allow to cool.

9. To assemble the pot, pipe gingerbread-coloured royal icing on the underside of one of the red rings of gingerbread.

10. Then taking care not to touch or smudge the royal icing, turn it over and position it on the base.

11. Repeat the process with a classic gingerbread ring.

12. Fix the rings in alternate colours with royal icing until they are all in place. Allow to dry.

13. To assemble the lid, fix the largest of the three remaining circles to the centre of the underside of the lid with royal icing to form the keeper.

14. Turn the lid over to the top side and fix the red circle and the small classic gingerbread circle to form the handle. Allow to dry.

Ring box

To make an engagement ring box, use the same construction techniques as above, but replace the circles with hearts using the cutters listed on page 83. The lid uses the inlay baking technique seen on pages 56–57.

Tip

You can now fill the pots with your favourite treats. If you are making these pots as gifts, you can fix the lid onto the pot after it has been filled, with a few small spots of royal icing. This will hold the lid in place, but it can also be easily removed.

KRANSEKAKE

Based on a classic Scandinavian confection, this gingerbread *kransekake* forms a stunning, delicious and beautifully scented centrepiece to any special celebration.

A traditional *kransekake* is made with a dough that combines ground almonds and whisked egg whites. This is baked into a series of overlapping concentric rings using a special set of tins. The rings are then stacked into a cone and decorated to create a wonderful *kransekake*.

Our *kransekake* is made from gingerbread, so we will make it differently. Instead of using tins to form the rings, we make and use a series of templates, and cut the gingerbread rings by hand. This may sound a little daunting but is in fact quite straightforward if you work accurately and methodically – the result is spectacular!

As gingerbread does not rise like traditional *kransekake* dough, you will need to bake two gingerbread rings of each size to give height. These rings are sandwiched together with chocolate before you stack and decorate your *kransekake*.

You will need:

- Your 'basic toolkit' (see pages 8, 10 and 13)
- 7 batches of classic gingerbread dough (see page 18)
- White royal icing
- 300g melted dark or milk chocolate
- Pizza wheel cutter
- Paring knife
- Piping bags
- Numbers 1.5 and 2 piping nozzles
- A4 – 210 × 297mm (8¼ × 11¾in) – paper or card
- Pencil
- 30cm (12in) round white iced cake board
- 15mm- (⁹⁄₁₆in-) wide ribbon
- 23cm (9in) cake board or tin (from which to measure the base)
- Templates (see pages 122–123)
- Cinnamon stick bundles, star anise and candied orange slices

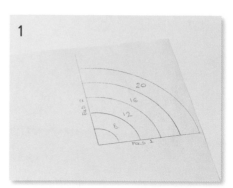

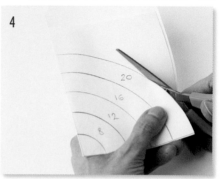

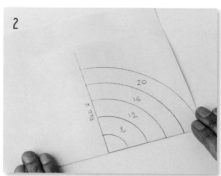

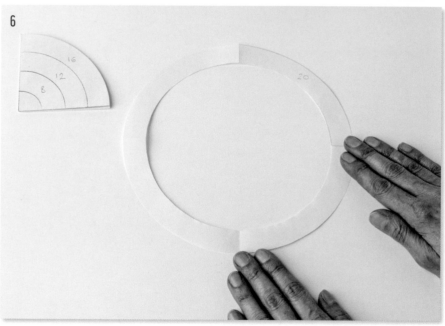

1. To make the templates, accurately trace or copy all four of the *kransekake* templates on pages 122–123 onto the top-right-hand corner of four separate sheets of A4 paper or card. Don't forget to number each ring according to size, as indicated on the templates. You will also need to transfer the labels indicating each fold.

2. Accurately fold each template sheet in half along fold line 1.

3. Then fold each sheet into quarters along fold line 2.

4. Keeping the template sheet folded, cut along the outer curved line and discard the excess paper.

5. Next, cut along the first curved line.

6. Carefully open out the cut section into a full ring and gently smooth out the creases.

7

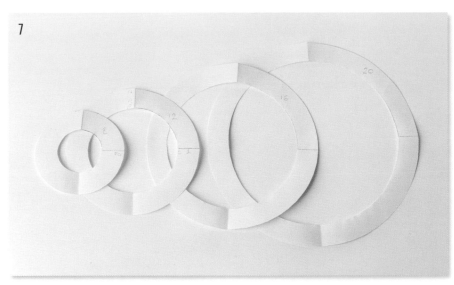

7. Repeat this process for all of the rings until you have a full set of fifteen concentric template rings.

8. Before rolling and cutting out the dough, experiment with grouping the template rings to find the most economical way of cutting as many rings as possible in one bake while leaving enough space between each ring to allow for expansion. Many of the smaller rings can be positioned inside the larger ones to save space. This will depend on the size of your baking sheet and oven. You will need to bake two rings of each size.

9. Roll out a large sheet of classic gingerbread dough on baking parchment or a silicone mat using the 3mm spacers. Apply vegetable shortening liberally to the underside of each group of template rings before placing them on the dough in the spacing decided on in step 8. Then cut around them with a pizza wheel cutter and remove the excess dough.

10. Bake all of the shapes and allow to cool. Repeat this process until you have cut out and baked all of the rings. There should be thirty rings in total. Arrange the matching pairs of rings in size order with their undersides together. Lastly, roll out, cut and bake a 23cm (9in) circle of gingerbread dough for the base.

8

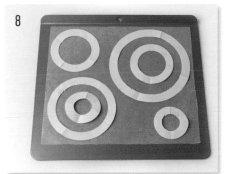

9

10

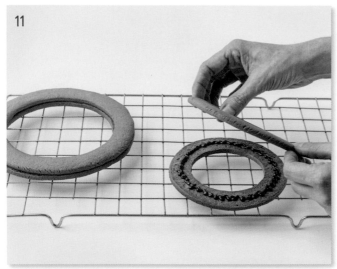

11

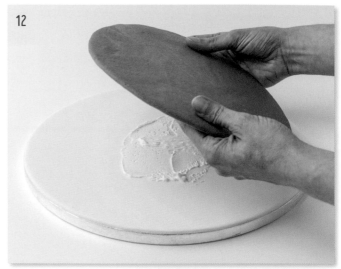

12

13

14

15

11. Pipe a line of melted chocolate on the underside of one of each pair of gingerbread rings and position and fix the matching gingerbread ring in place. Fix each pair of rings together and allow the chocolate to set.

12. Assemble the *kransekake* by first spreading a little royal icing onto an iced cake board (see page 30) and fixing the gingerbread base in place.

13. Pipe snail's trail bead piping (see page 34) using a number 2 piping nozzle and white royal icing around the base to neaten the edge.

14. Pipe dots of royal icing onto one side of the largest ring and fix to the base.

15. Pipe a continuous wavy line of white royal icing using a number 1.5 piping nozzle around the top of the ring.

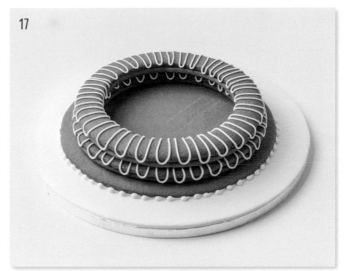

16. Lower the next-sized ring in place while the royal icing is still wet. Hold the ring from the inside so as not to smudge the piping when you remove your fingers.

17. Pipe the top of the ring as before.

18. Repeat this process until all of the rings are in place and allow to set before moving the *kransekake*.

19. Decorate the *kransekake* with cinnamon stick bundles, star anise and candied orange slices – the recipe for which can be found on page 24 – and trim the cake drum edge with 15mm-(⁹⁄₁₆in-) wide ribbon.

CHRISTMAS TREE COOKIE CAKE

Delight your family and friends with this fun and festive Christmas cake. Snow-white and sky-blue icing decorated with flood-iced fir trees will transform your favourite cake recipe into a winter wonderland!

〈〈〈〈〈〈〈〈

You will need:

- Your 'basic toolkit' (see pages 8, 10 and 13)
- One 15cm- (6in-) round, 13cm- (5in-) deep, triple-layer pale blue iced cake
- 20cm- (8in-) round white iced cake drum
- 1 batch of classic gingerbread dough (see page 18)
- 75 × 40mm Christmas tree cookie cutter
- White royal icing
- Red, green and brown flood icing
- White modelling paste
- Parallel wheel cutter
- Cornflour (corn starch) dusting bag
- Piping bags
- Number 1.5 piping nozzle
- Artists' paintbrush
- 15mm- (⅝in-) width ribbon of your choice
- Three 150mm- (6in-) long white paper lollipop sticks

1. Roll out a sheet of classic gingerbread dough on baking parchment or a silicone mat using the 3mm spacers. Cut out thirteen Christmas tree shapes. Bake and allow to cool.

93

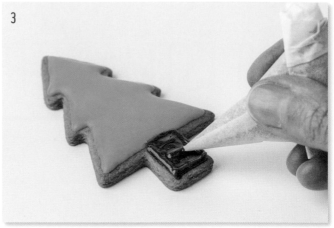

2. Fix your iced cake onto the white iced cake drum with royal icing. Lightly dust your work surface with cornflour (corn starch) and roll and cut a 20mm- (¾in-) wide and 5mm- (¼in-) thick ribbon of white modelling paste long enough to go around the cake, using the parallel wheel cutter. Fix the sugar ribbon in place with a little water and trim off any excess paste.

3. Following the instructions on page 35, flood-ice six of the gingerbread trees in red, and seven in green. Then flood-ice the tree trunks in brown and allow to dry.

4. Pipe a series of diagonal lines and dots using a number 1.5mm piping nozzle onto the green trees.

5. Outline and pipe vertical lines on the tree trunks.

6. Pipe lines to form branches onto the red trees and the line marking onto the trunks as before. Allow to dry.

7. Fix five trees of each colour alternately around the side of the cake with royal icing.

8. Pipe small white royal iced dots onto the blue icing to resemble falling snow using a number 1.5 piping nozzle.

9. Fix lollipop sticks to the backs of the three remaining trees with dots of royal icing and allow to dry.

10. Position two green trees on top of the cake by inserting the lollipop sticks into the cake.

11. Finally, position the last red tree.

WEDDING CAKE

This stunning cake design forms a heartwarming centrepiece to a very special celebration.

Gingerbread and cake: well there's nothing more to add – the combination speaks for itself! Bake your favourite cake recipe or the delicious ginger cake recipe on page 22

This three-tier cake comprises one 13cm (5in), one 18cm (7in) and one 23cm (9in) round cake, each 10cm (4in) deep; however, you can adapt the size and depth of the tiers to suit any number of guests. Even with a single tier, this cake is stunning.

You will need:

- Your 'basic toolkit' (see pages 8, 10 and 13)
- 1 batch of classic gingerbread dough (see page 18)
- One 13cm (5in), one 18cm (7in) and one 23cm (9in) round, white iced triple-layer cakes, iced on hardboards of the same size as each tier
- 30cm (12in) round white iced cake board
- 15mm- (⁹⁄₁₆in-) wide ribbon
- White modelling paste
- White royal icing
- Piping bags
- Numbers 1.5 and 3 piping nozzles
- Gingerbread figure cutters (or use the templates on page 126)
- 10mm and 15mm circle cutters
- 80 × 65mm gingerbread figure cutter
- 10mm, 35mm and 50mm five-petal flower cutters
- Scribing tool
- 150mm (6in-) long white paper lollipop sticks

1. Roll out a sheet of classic gingerbread dough on baking parchment or a silicone mat using the spacers. Cut out four 50mm (2in) flower shapes with 15mm (³⁄₈in) circles cut out of the centre, five 35mm (1³⁄₈in) flower shapes with 10mm circles cut out of the middle and eighteen 10mm (³⁄₈in) flower shapes using a number 3 piping nozzle to cut circles out of the middle. Cut two figures from the gingerbread dough. Bake and allow to cool.

2. Pipe an outline on the flower shapes in white royal icing using the number 1.5 piping nozzle and allow to dry.

3. Trace the gingerbread people patterns on page 126 onto baking parchment, or design your own characters. Then prick the design onto each figure using the method on page 47.

4. Pipe over the prick markings with white royal icing using the same nozzle as before and allow to dry. Fix a small flower shape onto each figure with royal icing.

5. Dowel and stack the cake tiers onto the 30cm (12in) cake board. Fix them in place with white royal icing and trim the cake board edge with your choice of 15mm- (⅝in-) wide ribbon. Next, make the rope twist trims by first rolling two long strings of white modelling paste of the same length.

6. Twist the strings together to form a rope twist.

7

Tip

You may have to make more than one length of rope twist to achieve enough length to go round the larger tiers. In that case, try to position the ends at the sides or backs of the tiers. Match the joins and neaten them with royal icing so that they appear continuous.

7. Position a rope twist around the base of each tier with its ends meeting at the back of the cake. Fix each rope twist with a little water applied with an artists' paintbrush.

8. Position and fix the flower shapes on the front of the cake with a little white royal icing to form a cascade.

9. Fix lollipop sticks onto the backs of the figures with royal icing. Allow the icing to dry before inserting the lollipop sticks to position the figures on top of the cake.

8

9

PICTURE PURR-FECT

Warm and cosy gingerbread cats look out of the bedroom window at the moon and stars on a crisp winter's night. If you listen carefully, you can almost hear them purring. This delightful project creates a wonderful decoration – and a purr-fect gift.

This project requires some accurate cutting for the fuse baking, three shades of gingerbread, and some shortbread for the moon and stars.

You will need:

- Your 'basic toolkit' (see pages 8, 10 and 13)
- 1 batch of classic gingerbread dough (see page 18)
- 1½ batches of dark treacle gingerbread dough (see page 19)
- Half a batch of pale gingerbread dough (see page 19)
- 1½ batches chocolate gingerbread dough (see page 19)
- Quarter batch of shortbread dough (see page 19)
- Scissors
- Pizza wheel cutter
- Sugarcraft wheel cutter
- Paring knife
- Smooth long bladed knife
- Metal ruler
- Vegetable shortening
- Numbers 1 and 2 piping nozzles
- Black royal icing and gingerbread-coloured royal icing
- 15mm star cutter
- 30mm and 45mm circle cutters
- Templates (see pages 124–125)

Tip

Gingerbread dough does not seem to spread as much when baked on a silicone mat as it does on baking parchment, making a silicone mat ideal for baking this project. If you don't have a silicone mat, the project can be baked on baking parchment, but the results may not be as accurate.

1. The first steps of this project will form the base of the picture that comprises the window frame, window sill and the walls. Prepare the templates for this: copy and enlarge the templates on page 124. Cut out the window and glazing bar section and apply vegetable shortening to the underside of the template. Roll out a sheet of classic gingerbread on baking parchment or a silicone mat to a thickness of 2mm (¹⁄₁₆in). Cut around the shape using a long smooth bladed knife. Use the template when cutting out this first shape as the window needs to be higher on the mat, allowing more space at the bottom for the sill and the wall.

2. Carefully cut away the window sections from the template except for the cross glazing bars; place the template for the cross glazing bars accurately on the dough.

3. Cut around the cross glazing bar template, leaving the four windows around the template intact.

4. Remove the template.

5. Remove the dough from the cross glazing bars section with a paring knife.

6. Roll a large sheet of treacle gingerbread dough on baking parchment to a thickness of 2mm (¹⁄₁₆in). Measure the width of the space where the glazing bars will go and cut two strips of dough to the same width and 220mm (8¾in) long. Place the strips in the refrigerator for 20 minutes to firm, and make them easier to handle, then carefully inlay them into the cross section.

7. Remove the little piece of dough in the middle where the two strips cross.

8. Trim any excess at the ends of the strips.

9. Cut a further two strips of treacle gingerbread dough 10 × 220mm (⅜ × 8¾in) to form the window frame. Position on the top and bottom of the window.

10. Straighten the edges by lightly pressing a ruler against the sides, then trim any excess dough.

11. Roll a small sheet of pale gingerbread dough on baking parchment to a thickness of 2mm (1⁄16in) and cut out a 25 × 250mm (1 × 9¾in) strip; then position this along the bottom of the shape. Straighten and remove the excess as before.

12. Cut from treacle gingerbread dough a further two strips 50 × 250mm (2 × 9¾in) and two that are 25 × 350mm (1 × 13¾in). Place the shorter and wider strips on the top and bottom of the shape, trim the excess then place the longer stripes down both sides. Trim and straighten as before. Bake and allow to cool.

13. Next, roll a large sheet of chocolate gingerbread dough on baking parchment to a thickness of 2mm (1⁄16in). Cut four strips 25 × 360mm (1 × 14¼in) to form the frame. Using the template as a guide, position the strips onto a silicone mat to form a rectangle, ensuring that it is the same size as the template. Mitre the ends by cutting them at 45° angles using a paring knife. Bake and flip as before between two wire racks to prevent damage to the baked frame.

14. Roll as before and cut out two curtains from treacle gingerbread dough using the template on page 125. Emboss folds in the curtains with a sugarcraft wheel cutter.

Tip

As the gingerbread is large and fragile, it is better to flip the baked piece upside down between two wire racks, peel away the mat, then flip it upright to cool. If you try to remove the baked piece from the mat by hand or use a palette knife, it may damage the piece.

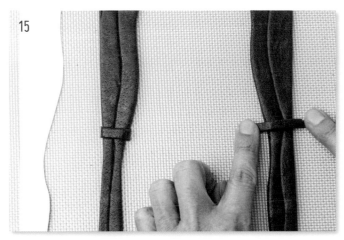

15. Cut two narrow strips of dough 7mm (¼in) wide to form the tie-backs, lay the strips across each curtain and trim the excess. Bake and allow to cool.

16. Roll as before and cut the two cats from chocolate gingerbread dough using the cat templates and a pizza wheel cutter or paring knife. You will also need to cut the moon using a 45mm circle cutter, and removing a small section using a 30mm circle cutter to form a crescent and three 15mm stars from shortbread dough. Finally cut a 7mm × 205mm (¼ × 8in) strip for the curtain pole from treacle gingerbread dough. Bake and allow to cool.

17. Assemble the picture fixing the pieces onto the background using gingerbread-coloured royal icing and the number 2 piping nozzle. Due to expansion during baking, some of the pieces such as the curtains and curtain pole may need to be trimmed a little to fit neatly in place.

18. Finally, pipe the cats' whiskers with black royal icing using a number 1 piping nozzle. Allow to dry before moving or hanging up the picture.

GINGERBREAD HOUSE

This charming gingerbread house can be decorated in a number of ways and made in different sizes if you simply alter the templates.

You will need:

- Your 'basic toolkit' (see pages 8, 10 and 13)
- 3 batches of classic gingerbread dough (see page 18)
- 1 batch of red gingerbread dough (see pages 20–21)
- 20cm (8in) white iced cake board
- 15mm- (⁹⁄₁₆in-) wide ribbon
- Straight scalloped edge frill cutter
- Small wheel cutter
- Paring knife
- Long kitchen knife
- Long serrated knife
- 10mm and 20mm heart cutters
- White royal icing
- Gingerbread-coloured royal icing
- Piping bags
- Numbers 1, 1.5 and 2 piping nozzles
- Long glass-headed pins (such as hat pins)
- Small jars or bottles (optional, for propping up panels during construction)
- Vegetable shortening
- Templates (see page 126)

1. Copy or trace the house templates on page 126 and cut them out. Cover the underside of each template with vegetable shortening and set aside. Roll out a sheet of classic and a sheet of red gingerbread dough on baking parchment using 3mm spacers. Then cut three 30 × 220mm (1³⁄₁₆ × 8¾in) strips of each colour for each of the two roof panels, cutting one edge with the scalloped edge frill cutter and the other with a long kitchen knife. If possible, set the trimmings aside.

2. Layer the alternating coloured strips with the scalloped edges offset to form roof tiles. Ensure the overlaps are spaced so that the completed panel is the same width as the roof template.

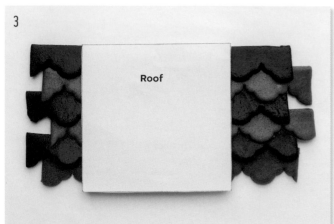

3

Roof

4

5

3. Create a roof template from card – it is a simple 105 × 105mm (4⅛ × 4⅛in) square. Place the roof template over the overlaid dough strips ensuring that it is in a landscape position.

4. Trim the ends of the overlaid strips to form the first roof panel. Then cut the second roof panel, ensuring that the template is laid on the overlaid dough strips in the same position as the first so that the end scallops are roughly even on both panels.

5. To make the barge boards, roll two 50 × 160mm (2 × 6¼in) strips of red gingerbread dough and classic gingerbread dough to a thickness of 2mm (1⁄16in) or gently roll the trimmings set aside in step 1 so they are a little thinner. Align and layer the dough strips or trimmings in alternating colours to form a layered sheet. Place in the refrigerator for an hour to firm. Trim the ends and one side of the layered sheet; neaten, then cut four 2mm (1⁄16in) strips from its length.

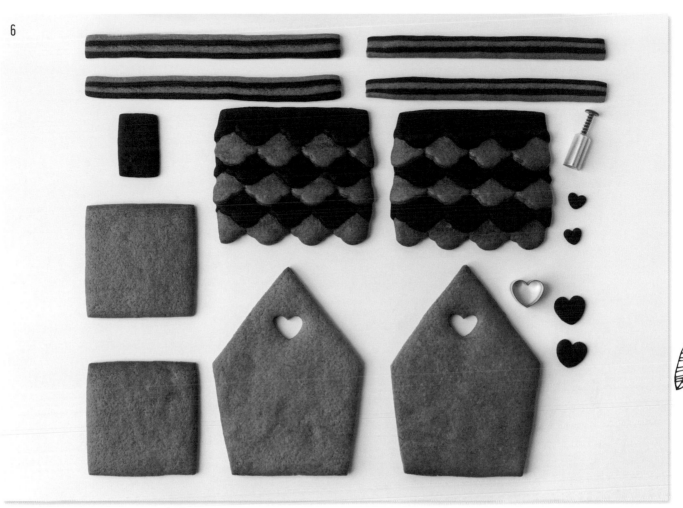

6. Roll a large sheet of classic gingerbread dough and a smaller sheet of red gingerbread dough using 3mm spacers and cut the front and back panels using the templates on page 126. Cut a 20mm heart from the same position in each panel as shown on the template. Next cut two side panels from classic gingerbread dough. Then cut two 10mm hearts, two 20mm hearts and a 25 × 40mm (1 × 1⁹⁄₁₆in) rectangle from red gingerbread dough for the decorations and front door. Bake and allow to cool.

7. Use a serrated knife to trim the ends of the roof panels, the bottom edges of the front two panels and the side and bottom edges of the side panels.

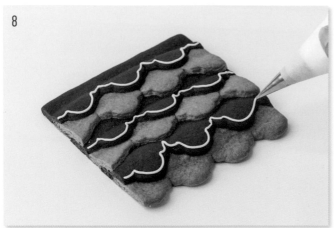

8. Decorate the roof panels by outlining the scallops with white royal icing using a number 1.5 piping nozzle.

9. Next, pipe fleur-de-lys shapes on each of the red scallops using a number 1.5 nozzle.

10. Pipe dots onto the classic gingerbread scallops using a number 1 nozzle.

11. Trace the front and side panel decorations onto baking parchment and prick out the design onto the end and side panels. Then use a 1.5 piping nozzle to pipe over the guide markings with white royal icing. Fix the small red hearts into place with gingerbread-coloured royal icing and allow to dry.

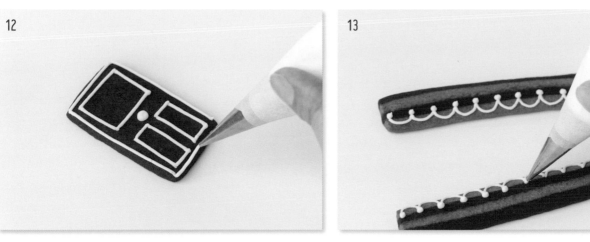

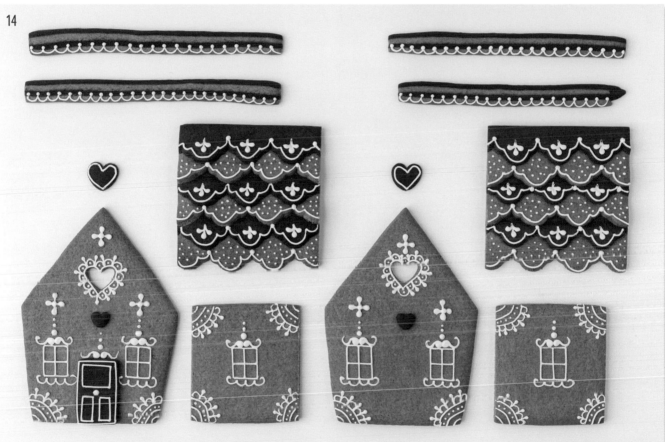

12. Pipe the door panels and handle onto the front door and outline the two larger red hearts with white royal icing and a number 1.5 piping nozzle.

13. Finally, decorate the four barge boards with a scalloped line topped with little dots using a number 1.5 piping nozzle and white royal icing, ensuring that you pipe along the same colour edge on each of the barge boards. Allow to dry.

14. Fix the front door onto the front panel with gingerbread-coloured royal icing and lay out all of the panels ready for assembly.

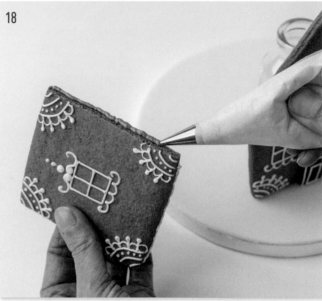

15. Lightly mark out where the first panel is going to be positioned on the iced drum board using the paper templates as a guide. Have a few small bottles or jars on hand to support the panels while they dry.

16. Pipe a generous line of white royal icing onto the bottom edge of the front panel.

17. Fix the front panel to the board, propping it up with a bottle or jar.

18. Pipe a generous line of gingerbread-coloured royal icing onto the edge of one of the side panels, making sure the panel is the correct way up.

19

20

21

22

23

19. Fix the side panel to the front panel and support it with another jar. Use a set square to ensure the front and side are at a right angle.

20. Repeat this process for the other side and back, supporting each panel with a bottle or jar. Remove any excess royal icing that may have squeezed out and allow the panels joins to dry.

21. Remove the bottle from inside the house and reinforce the internal walls join and where the bottom edges of the wall panels meet the iced drum with a generous amount of gingerbread coloured royal icing.

22. Neaten the exterior side join by piping vertical lines of snail's trail bead piping (see page 34) using white royal icing and a number 2 piping nozzle.

23. Pipe snail's trail bead piping to neaten the base of the house.

24. Pipe a generous amount of gingerbread-coloured royal icing on the top edges of the end panels.

25. Fix the roof panels in position and secure them temporarily by gently inserting four clean glass-headed pins through the roof and front and back wall panels while the icing dries. Ensure that the pins are angled inwards slightly.

26. Pipe a generous line of gingerbread-coloured royal icing along the top of the roof, then reinforce the ridge join.

27. Next, measure the barge boards by holding them against the roof to see how long they need to be and lightly mark an angled line where both barge boards will meet to create a neat vertical join.

28. Cut the ends of the barge boards along the marked lines so they form a neat vertical join at the roof apex

29. Fix each in place with gingerbread-coloured royal icing

30. Fix the hearts in place with gingerbread royal icing. Once the roof and the barge boards have dried and feel secure, remove the four pins and store them safely out of the kitchen.

31. Make a length of rope twist using white modelling paste using the same technique as on page 98. Measure the space between the front and back barge boards and cut the rope to the required length. Fix in place with white royal icing.

32. Finally, trim the cake board edge with your choice of 15mm- (⅝in-) wide ribbon.

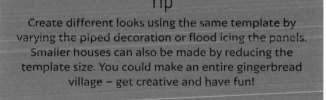

Tip
Create different looks using the same template by varying the piped decoration or flood icing the panels. Smaller houses can also be made by reducing the template size. You could make an entire gingerbread village – get creative and have fun!

Gingerbread House variations

Gingerbread houses can be made in any flavoured or coloured gingerbread doughs of your choice – you could even decorate them with flood icing on the walls and roofs, as seen on the house opposite.

TEMPLATES

*All templates are produced at full size
(100%) unless otherwise stated.*

Piped Snowflake Cookies
pages 46–49

Piped Snowflake Cookies

pages 46–49

Christmas Tree

pages 70–73

Tree and trunk.

The base template is a circle with a diameter of 15cm (6in).

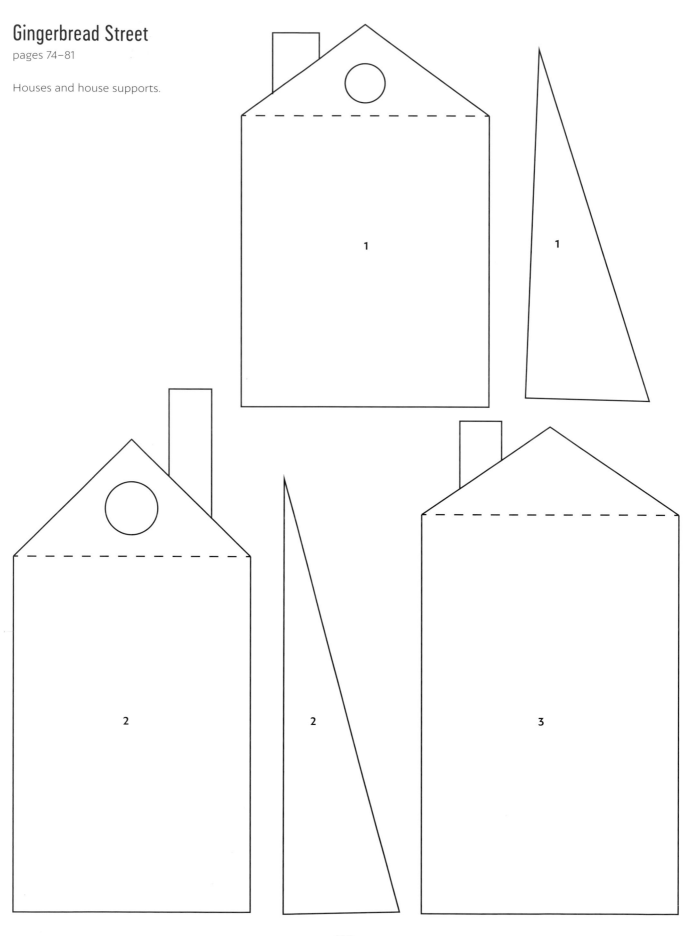

Gingerbread Street

pages 74–81

Houses and house supports.

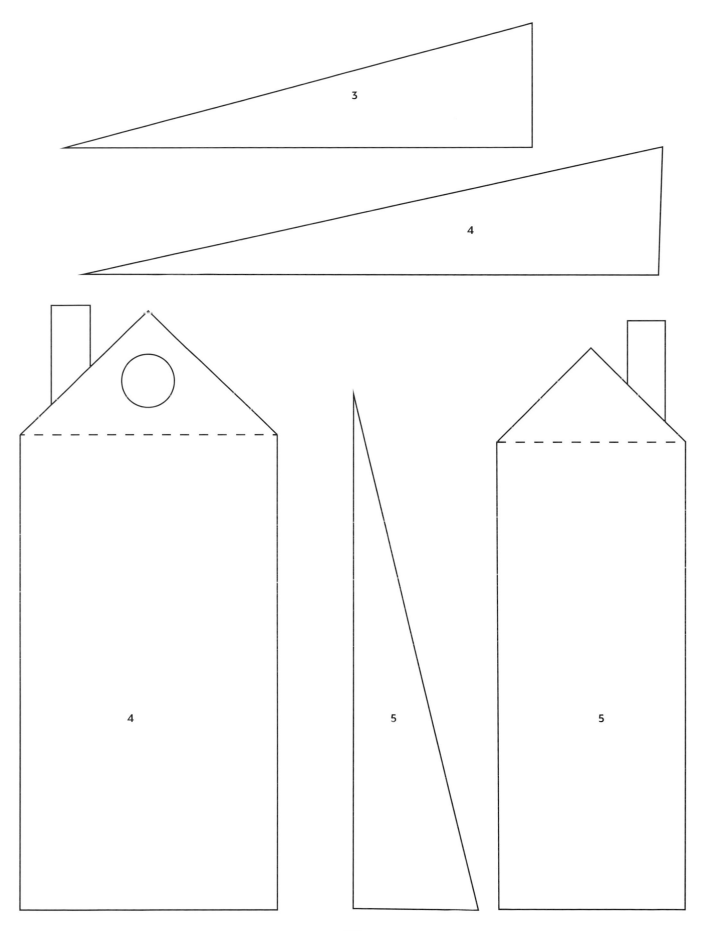

Kransekake

pages 86–91

The numbers on each ring relate to its circumference in cm. The imperial conversions are listed in the table below.

cm	in
1	½
2	¾
3	1¼
4	1½
5	2
6	2¼
7	2¾
8	3¼
9	3½
10	4
11	4¼
12	4¾
13	5
14	5½
15	6
16	6¼
17	6¾
18	7
19	7½
20	8

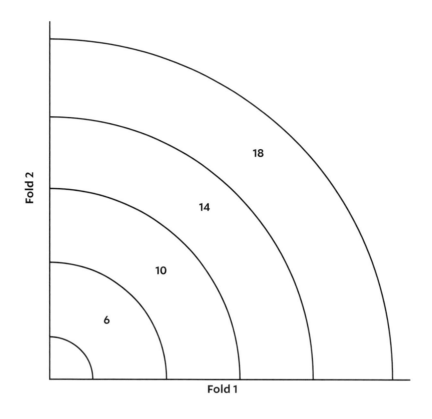

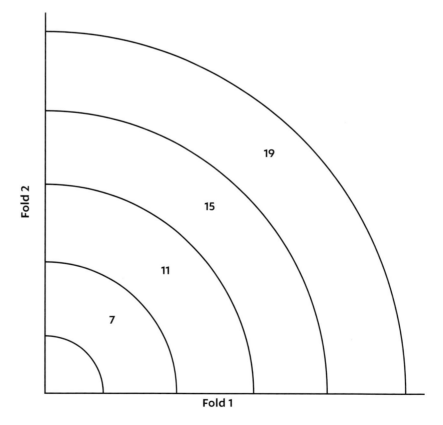

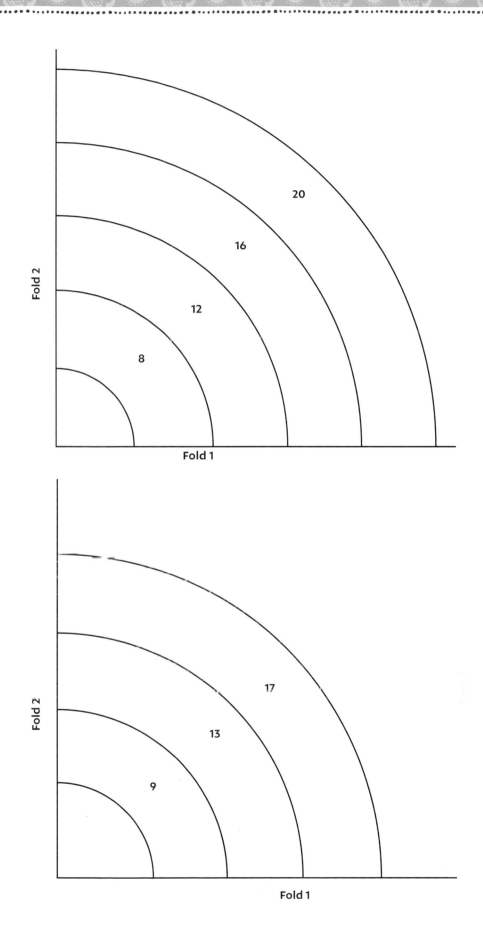

Fold 2

Fold 1

20

16

12

8

Fold 2

Fold 1

17

13

9

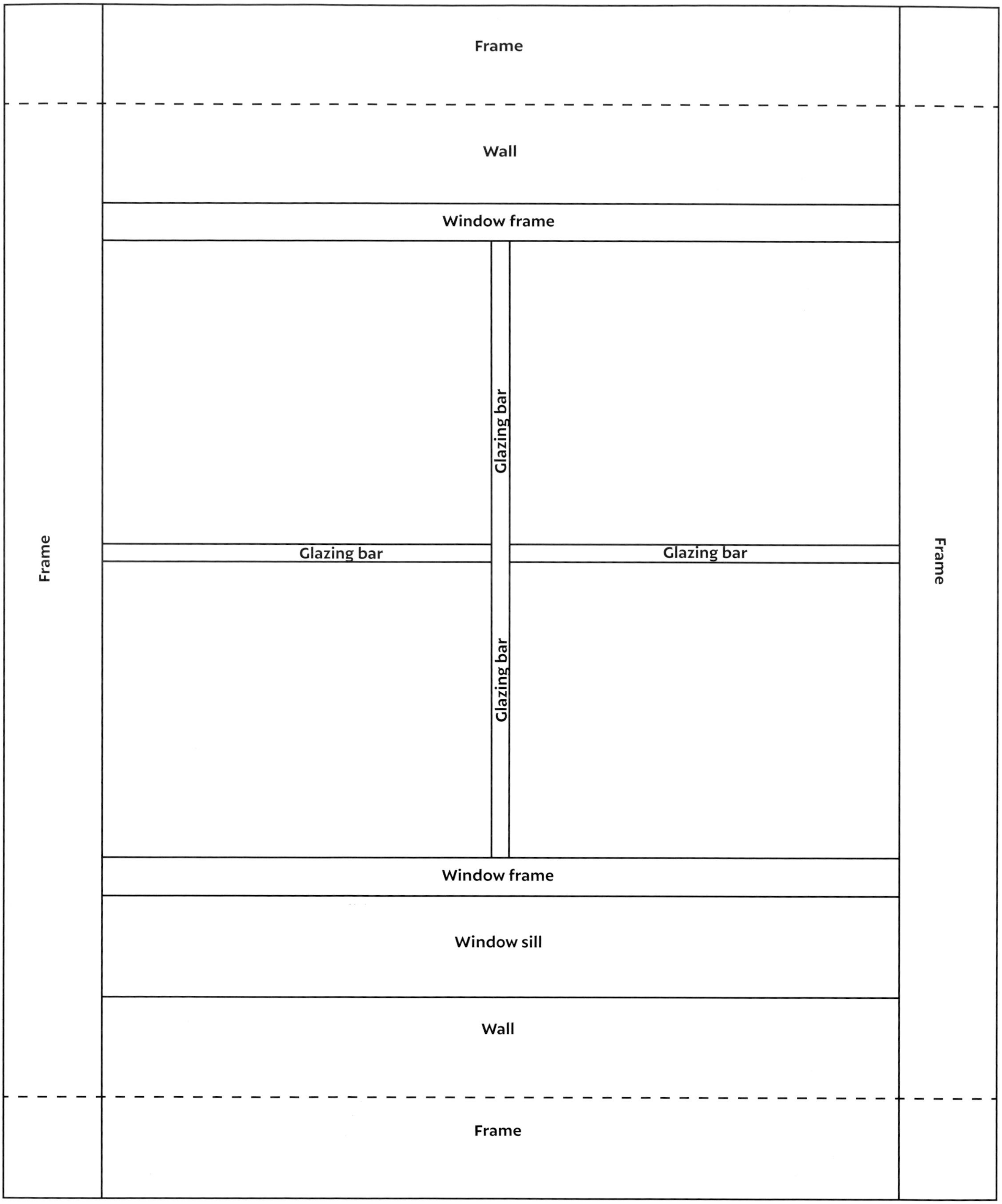

Frame

Wall

Window frame

Frame

Glazing bar

Glazing bar

Glazing bar

Glazing bar

Frame

Window frame

Window sill

Wall

Frame

Picture Purr-fect

pages 100–105

Cat templates.

Opposite

Picture Purr-fect

pages 100–105

Window template.
This template has been reproduced here at 75%. Photocopy the template at 133% to use it at its full size.

Curtain.
This template has been reproduced here at 75%. Photocopy the template at 133% to use it at its full size; cut out one curtain, then flip over the template to cut out a second, mirror-image curtain shape from the gingerbread.

Wedding Cake

pages 96–99

Gingerbread House

pages 106–117

Front and back. Cut out two.

Sides. Cut out two.

Gingerbread House

pages 106–117

The roof panels are squares of 10.5 × 10.5cm (4⅛ × 4⅛in). Cut two for each house from gingerbread dough.

CONVERSION TABLES

WEIGHT: GRAMS (G) TO OUNCES (OZ)

g	5	10	15	20	25	30	35	40	45	50	55	60	65	70	75	80
oz	⅛	⅜	½	¾	⅞	1	1¼	1⅜	1⅝	1¾	2	2⅛	2¼	2½	2⅝	2⅞

g	85	90	95	100	105	110	115	120	125	130	135	140	145	150	155	160
oz	3	3⅛	3⅜	3½	3¾	3⅞	4	4¼	4⅜	4⅝	4¾	5	5⅛	5¼	5½	5⅝

g	165	170	175	180	185	190	195	200	205	210	215	220	225	230	235	240
oz	5⅞	6	6⅛	6⅜	6½	6¾	6⅞	7	7¼	7⅜	7⅝	7¾	7⅞	8⅛	8¼	8½

g	245	250	255	260	265	270	275	280	285	290	295	300	305	310	315	320
oz	8⅝	8⅞	9	9⅛	9⅜	9½	9¾	9⅞	10	10¼	10⅜	10⅝	10¾	10⅞	11⅛	11¼

g	325	330	335	340	345	350	355	360	365	370	375	380	385	390	395	400
oz	11½	11⅝	11⅞	12	12⅛	12⅜	12½	12¾	12⅞	13	13¼	13⅜	13⅝	13¾	13⅞	14⅛

g	405	410	415	420	425	430	435	440	445	450	455	460	465	470	475	480
oz	14¼	14½	14⅝	14⅞	15	15⅛	15⅜	15½	15¾	15⅞	16	16¼	16⅜	16⅝	16¾	16⅞

g	485	490	495	500												
oz	17⅛	17¼	17½	17⅝												

VOLUME: MILLILITRES (ML) TO FLUID OUNCES (FL.OZ)

Note: This table contains measurements applied to recipes in this book.

ml	25	70	100	125	150	280	300	500	900
fl.oz	⅞	2½	3½	4½	5¼	9¾	10½	17½	31¾

INDEX